A Programmer's Tale (1966-2001)

Ralph Atenasio

ISBN 978-0-6152-0362-1

Dedication

I dedicate this book to my three children, Christopher, David and Lisa. As much as I looked forward each day going to work and building cool software products, coming home to my family each night was a much greater source of joy. And as much as I feel I've accomplished in my career, no work accomplishment can compare to the sense of accomplishment I feel for having raised three great kids.

- Contents -

Introduction

Life is a series of adventures, both big and small. This book chronicles my series of adventures during the thirty five years I spent working as a computer programmer and software engineer. My career began in 1966 when mainstream computing was still in its infancy, and ended in 2001, not long after the dot-com/telecom bubble burst forcing scores of software engineers either to retire or start new careers.

My adventures took me from coast to coast as well as to a number of different foreign countries. I've worked for a two-person company, a very large federal government organization, and all sizes of companies in between. I started as an individual contributor, logged time as a software manager, became a contract software engineer, built and attempted to market several products of my own, and finished my career at an Internet startup with the promise of becoming a millionaire through a generous stock option.

I worked on all sizes of systems from handheld devices to mainframes as well as complex multiprocessor-based communications systems and on all levels of software from low-level hardware device drivers to end-user business applications. I preferred working on smaller machines and moved to mini and micro based systems as they came upon the scene. I enjoyed not only the complexities of operating system internals, but also the challenge of making complex systems easy for the non-technical or non-computer literate end user to understand.

I spent the last ten or so years of my career in the area of communications and networking – allowing computers to communicate with each other over all sorts of communications links. Other applications I worked on over the years included data collection, data processing (i.e. Inventory Control, Accounts Receivable), word processing, security (encryption, authentication), multi-tasking operating systems, and drivers for all sorts of peripherals. And there was that mini-based dog track system that I implemented.

I learned a lot during those thirty five years, mostly through successes, but also through some painful failures. I constantly sought ways to improve my craft, my productivity, and the quality of my product. I learned my strengths and weaknesses and used that knowledge to help guide my journey.

Having worked in different countries (Germany, Great Britain and Costa Rica), I experienced and enjoyed learning how cultural differences affected the workplace, and having worked in the industry for such a long time, I experienced firsthand the dramatic advances in hardware and software that took place in the industry over the years.

In this book I describe, in chronological order, all the software projects I have worked on, with a goal of recounting what I learned from each project (the good, the bad, and the ugly). I examine the 'why' for both my successes and failures. I talk about the changes in the working environment that have taken place over the years, both in terms of advances made in software development methods/productivity, as well as changes I noticed in the social environment within the workplace. In the first part of the book, there is more 'project description' and less 'opinion'. That ratio changes towards the end of the book where I explain what I think are some the better ways of developing, and (more important) managing, software. The longer I spent in the industry, the more I learned and the more opinions I acquired – many of which are now quite strong. I talk about some of the problems I see in the industry today and suggest some remedies.

I've had an interesting career, working on many interesting projects and living in many interesting places and I hope the description of my experiences and adventures, with some personal anecdotes thrown in, will make this book an enjoyable read.

The target audience for this book is everyone involved in, or thinking of becoming involved in, the world of software development, including those who manage software people. It should also appeal to those who have been in the industry for a while and have had similar experiences. All of us who managed to stay in the software industry over the last forty or so years have had unique experiences. This book describes mine.

Chapter 1

Returning to the Real World

February 1965. I climbed onto a bus that would take me from McGuire Air Force Base to the airport for a flight back home. I had just finished four years in the Air Force, the last two and a half spent in Berlin, Germany. I remember sitting on the bus with a feeling of exhilaration. Free at last of the autocratic rule of the military. I took off my Air Force cap knowing that I would never have to put it on again. It's not that I didn't enjoy the last four years, especially the last two and a half, but during those four years I realized that I did not respond well to authority, especially when those in authority were not particularly competent. Most of those I worked for were very competent and had the respect of those that worked for them, but those few that weren't could make life very difficult.

I was also glad to be done with those dirty jobs that came with the territory such as 5AM Kitchen Police (KP) or cleaning bathrooms messed up by GI's who had been out drinking all night. I knew that if I had re-enlisted, those undesirable chores would have eventually disappeared as I moved up in rank, but the authority issue kept me from staying in the Air Force. It's too bad because I enjoyed the work. As I sat on that bus on the first leg of my trip home, I wondered what I would do for the rest of my life. I didn't have a clue.

After graduating from high school, there was no money in the family budget for college. I could have gone to work in my father's dry cleaning business, and take it over one day, but after years of helping out in the business, I knew it wasn't for me. Every week the same routine: pick up the clothes, have them cleaned, press them, sort them, and deliver them. I don't know how my father did it all those years. I think what kept him going was his visits and chats with the many customers on his multi-city delivery route.

My first job after high school was as an accountant's assistant (check sorter) in a large Boston bank. While there, I decided to check out the educational opportunities in the Air Force. I took their battery of entrance exams and scored high in electronics. I was promised training and a job in the field of electronics. During basic training I was shown a list of my follow-on training possibilities. On the top of the list was a 52-week course in missile maintenance in Amarillo, Texas. Second was a 38-week course in missile maintenance at another base somewhere in Texas. Sounded good to me.

Before basic training was completed, however, I was asked to take a test to check out my ability to learn a foreign language. I guess I passed because I was then asked if I wanted to become an Air Force linguist. I would attend a university, study a language for nine months, and get 23 college credits. At first I declined the offer because I was excited about my career in the field of electronics. Also, I really didn't feel that I was capable of learning another language. I flunked out of Italian in high school, and I'm Italian. But they talked me into it. (I was told later by an airman who did turn down the offer that they just kept him at Lackland Air Force Base, the Air Force's 'basic training' base, until he finally agreed.)

During that time period, most airmen selected to become linguists were sent to school to study Russian. I was one of a few selected to study Polish. Polish was perhaps not as interesting or as useful as Russian, but there was one major advantage - all duty stations for Polish linguists overseas were in Germany. Russian linguists could be sent to such places as Turkey or the Aleutian Islands in Alaska.

After nine months at Syracuse University studying intensive Polish for nine hours a day (6 hours classroom, 3 hours homework), I spent three months training as a Voice Intercept Operator in San Angelo, Texas, and then it was off to Berlin Germany for the rest of my 4-year tour.

The main airport in Berlin at that time, Tempelhof, which was in the heart of the city, was shared by the civilian airport and the US Air Force. Tempelhof became world known during the famous Berlin Airlift when the Soviets blocked land access to this island city behind the Iron Curtain. The building was designed by Hitler and was five stories high and five stories underground. It still had the scars of WWII. Many of the sub-ground levels were still flooded and unusable. There were still bullet holes on the building's façade. It was a semi-circular building about 1.2 kilometers in length. Our billets were there and the main NSA listening post with its array of antennas was at the end of the USAF side of the building.

Those were exciting times in Berlin. It was just about a year after the Wall went up. Both the Cuban Missile Crisis and the Kennedy assassination took place during my tour of duty. During the Cuban Missile Crisis, it was assumed that if we invaded Cuba, the Russians would retaliate by invading Berlin. We were located well behind the Iron Curtain, surrounded and greatly outnumbered. We didn't stand a chance. If invaded, our instructions were to destroy all classified information, put on civilian clothes, and blend in with the locals.

The Berliners loved JFK. When he died, many put single candles in their windows and lit them each evening. The day he came to Berlin and gave his famous "I am a Berliner" speech I slept late and missed it. A 'Berliner' was of course a resident of Berlin, but it was also the name of a local sweet resembling a jelly donut.

The work was always exciting. From Berlin, we could intercept and report on voice communications of the Russian, East German, Polish and Czech Air Forces. Some days we would only have to look up into the sky to know we were going to have a busy day. I enjoyed the work. I enjoyed living in Berlin. I just didn't enjoy being in the military.

After an exciting two and a half years in Berlin, returning home was a real downer. I was returning to a whole different world. Living in the encircled city was full of excitement and a certain amount of danger. I can't imagine what it's like to return from an active war zone. After returning to the home of my parents in the Boston suburbs, I just hung around for a while and helped out in my father's business. I went to the local unemployment agency to see if they had any jobs for a trained Polish Linguist. No luck! I collected unemployment checks for a while but helping out in the family business got old quick so I took a job at General Electric in the mailroom sorting mail. I guess my experience sorting bank checks helped me get this position. I still didn't have a clue as to what I wanted to do for the rest of my life.

One day I saw an ad in the Boston Globe for a Computer Programming course. I'm not sure why it interested me. I think it may have been because I'd be working with new languages. I had aced the Polish Language course at Syracuse, studied German in Germany, and now had confidence in my ability to learn languages. It was a 3-month course and we learned how to write programs for IBM's extremely successful 1401 computer (20,000 systems sold). The 1401 was a variable word machine with up to 16,000 bytes of core storage and supported peripherals included a card reader/punch, printer and magnetic tapes (no disk). It was used primarily for business applications such as payroll and accounts receivable.

After graduating, the school, Electronic Computer Programming Institute (ECPI), promised to help with job placement. That promise was never kept. After several months of searching for a job, the only offer I got was as a computer operator at MIT at $75 a week. I then wrote a letter to the National Security Agency (NSA) offering them both my old and new skills. Weeks after taking a day's worth of tests, including personality and polygraph tests, I was offered a job at NSA as a Polish Linguist, starting salary of $6800 a year. I put my aspirations of becoming a Computer Programmer on hold.

Chapter 2

Working for Uncle Sam

The National Security Agency is located at Ft. Meade, Maryland, which is about half way between Baltimore and Washington, D.C. It was about a 9-hour drive from my hometown in Massachusetts.

As soon as I got out of the military, I took all the money I saved while in Berlin and bought a 1960 red MGA roadster. I drove it to my computer programming course in Kenmore Square, Boston, every day. I usually parked it on Newbury Street, which was a back street very close to where ECPI was located. On one of my last days of class I returned to Newbury Street to find my little red roadster gone, never to be seen again.

My dad lent me enough money to buy an older (small oval rear window) VW bug. It got me to Maryland. Until I found a place to live, I stayed with a cousin who played first trumpet in the Navy Band and was living just outside of D.C. on the Pennsylvania Ave extension. It was December and it was already dark when I left NSA on my first day of work. Somehow I got totally lost on the way to my cousin's apartment. I ended up driving up and down Pennsylvania Ave in downtown D.C., driving by the White House a number of times without realizing it. I guess I expected it to be bigger and/or more impressive.

Once at NSA, I started attending the University of Maryland, evening division, working towards a degree in modern languages, building on my Polish language credits and some University of Maryland German language extension courses I took while in Berlin. At that time Computer Science degree programs were few and far between. My favorite courses were in the humanities (English lit, sociology, psychology) and my least favorite were the mandatory math courses. Algebra was okay, but I couldn't see how I would ever use what they were trying to teach me in calculus class. And I wanted to work with computers?

I spent a year in the languages group at NSA listening to tapes of Polish military or paramilitary organizations after which I would analyze and write intelligence reports on those organizations. Not very interesting. One of the highlights of that year was listening to a tape of a clandestine bug that was placed (probably by the CIA) in the bedroom of a high-ranking Polish military officer.

After a year in the languages group, I requested a transfer to a position where I could use my new computer programming skills. As a result of the Vietnam War, a new GI bill had come out. Uncle Sam would pay for my college education. So I told NSA that if they didn't let me transfer, I'd quit and go to college full time.

They transferred me to an office within the Languages Group, which provided computer support for that group. The office consisted mostly of data entry (key punch) operators but they also needed someone to write the occasional computer program. I remember writing a program in Fortran that read the contents of a magnetic tape searching for key words such as 'bomb'. I would also help out the girls with some of their data entry chores.

That job didn't last too long. The manager of the group was an ex-Army sergeant who at times thought he was still in the Army. One day he informed us that our office was to be visited by some VIPs and that we needed to have a clean-up. There was, of course, a cleaning crew that came in during the evenings and cleaned all the offices in the building. The data entry operators were to clean the equipment, and I, being the only guy in the group, was to lift up some of the heavy equipment during the floor cleaning process. I was a GG-7, which is equivalent to a captain in the military. I did my share of such jobs while in the Air Force. We often had to clean our work place, especially when we were going to have an inspection. Even if we had a busy night (lots of enemy planes flying), we had to stop working and start cleaning. "F..k the mission, clean the position". Well, I wasn't in the Air Force anymore and didn't have to follow these new orders.

A few days later I found myself in a small windowless room taking a 2-week course in how to operate a Hagelin Cipher Machine. It gave them some time to decide what to do with me next. I fortunately managed to get a job in the Computer Group where they had real programming positions. I was assigned to my first real programming project. It was an intelligence collection system that was in the initial stages of implementation. The hardware consisted of a midi-computer (Univac 1224A), a paper tape reader, six magnetic tapes, and a console keyboard/printer. The computer was about 5' high by 3' wide by 2' deep. It was a 24-bit machine with multiple rows of 24 lamps that were also buttons used for entering data in octal notation and for displaying results in octal notation directly to and from memory locations. It was quite something to watch an operator perform an assembly of a program by entering commands through the button lamps. It was like playing a musical instrument. And during a program assembly, we'd turn down the overhead lights and watch the light show displaying on the multi-colored button lamps.

All software was written in assembler language. Programs were entered through the system console's paper tape reader. Application input to the system was via a standalone high-speed paper tape reader. The input paper tapes were generated on morse code intercept positions. The text was read from paper tape and written to magnetic tape. One program would scan the data tape looking for key words such as 'bomba' or 'junta' (the system was installed in Panama). Reports would be generated and the tapes would be forwarded to NSA. Eventually I was the lead programmer on this project. One of the first changes I remember making was to allow the system to run with just four of the six tape drives. Previously, if one of the drives were down, the system wouldn't work. I don't remember now what all the tape drives were used for. Surely one was for programs, another for the captured data, and another for the keyword database.

Newer generation intelligence collection systems being worked on in our group used disks and cut out the manual paper tape operation. Data went directly from the intercept position into the computer.

I got to make three trips to Panama while working on this project. Interesting country. The first thing I remember seeing after deplaning was the local police, who looked more paramilitary than civilian in their green fatigues with their sub-machine guns slung over their shoulders. I also remember seeing small wooden huts scattered throughout the city that I believe were temporary holding cells used by the police.

On my second trip to Panama I was accompanied by a co-worker. After my first trip, I was determined not to drive in that city again (We would always stay in a hotel in Panama City instead of in the American Canal Zone). My co-worker was brave and agreed to drive the rental car. When we arrived he realized he had left his driver's license in the states. But he still did the driving. One day we were pulled over by one of those guys in fatigues with a machine gun over his shoulder. I don't remember why we were pulled over. We both got out of the car and went up to the guy in uniform. He was obviously asking for a driver's license. We were playing dumb. No comprendo. Unfortunately a bystander who spoke English came by and volunteered to help. In the confusion I took my driver's license out of my wallet, got behind my co-worker and pushed my hand holding the license into the small of his back. He got the hint and put his hand behind his back and grabbed my driver's license. Luckily, in those days driver's licenses did not have photos. For a short while I was picturing us inside one of those wooden holding cells.

Panama was incredibly humid. I visited an army barracks where they would hang their uniforms close to the ceiling, using poles to retrieve them. Better air circulation up there. One soldier had a pair of black dress shoes under his bed that he hadn't polished in a while. They had a layer of green mold on them. When it rained it poured so hard that some people in the city wouldn't bother with an umbrella or raincoat because it just didn't help much. Some would take cover, others would get a free bath.

I spent three years in the Computer Group at NSA working on the Panama project and several other smaller projects. It was time for a change. I missed Germany. I looked for an opportunity to work for the agency in Germany, but couldn't find a position for which I qualified. I was offered a position in Ethiopia, but politely turned it down. I probably could have gotten a position in England, but was determined to return to Germany. So I quit the agency and decided to go to Germany on my own and look for work.

One of the motivators for my wanting to leave the agency was their bureaucratic way of handling promotions. It reminded me of the military. During my stay in the Computer Group, I worked hard and accomplished a lot. During that same period there was a college grad who had been in our group about the same amount of time as I had. She would come to work and could spend a whole day going from desk to desk, chatting away and not accomplishing anything. When my GG-9 promotion finally came, she got hers at the same time. Our group was allotted a fixed number of GG-9 promotions for that promotion period. We were both next in the queue. I guess I wanted to prove to myself that I could make it in the business world where promotions were based more on merit than time in grade.

I look back fondly at my four years at NSA. I worked with a great bunch of people. We did lots together: parties, boat trips, ski trips. I still have some good friends from those days. And I don't want to give the wrong impression – most were extremely competent and hard working people. It's just that, probably like any government agency, there's a higher percentage of 'deadwood' than in the private sector.

I wasn't going to miss Maryland. Winters were somewhat less severe than Massachusetts, but not a lot. I had several encounters with black ice. Once while stopped on an NSA parking lot access road, which was pitched and sloping down towards the breakdown lane, my car (a 1967 Mustang Fastback at that time), slowly just slid sideways off the road. Clutching my steering wheel with both hands and pressing hard on the brakes didn't keep me from sliding sideways.

Another time I was driving home on the Baltimore-Washington Parkway after a late night of work and while driving at about 60 miles an hour, I spotted a big Cadillac sitting broadside on the highway in front of me. I applied the brakes, but absolutely no response. I accelerated and managed to swerve left of the car and after passing it, the Mustang started fishtailing violently from side to side. I ended up sliding onto the median strip and heading towards the lanes of oncoming traffic. Luckily the Mustang regained traction in the grass and I managed to steer it back onto the correct side of the highway. Never did stop.

As an aside, my car was insured with GEICO (Government Employees Insurance Co.). As far as I know, at that time one had to be a government employee to be insured with them. There were no GEICO geckos in those days.

In addition to mediocre weather, the area itself was not very exciting – not very close to the ocean nor the mountains. I would take a drive south into Virginia and the landscape would seem to immediately change becoming a lot greener and more interesting (less flat). One advantage the area did have was that it wasn't far from the nicer parts of Washington, D.C. like Georgetown. In those days, before it's downtown makeover, Baltimore was the pits.

Chapter 3

First Encounter with the Private Sector

I flew to Germany, bought a car ('66 VW bug), spent some time vacationing with friends, and set out to find a job. I interviewed with several Army CPO's (Civilian Personnel Offices) and with Univac in Frankfurt, but no luck. After about three months it was back to the states and to the Boston area. I brought a souvenir with me – a brand new VW bug. Luckily, the Boston area, where I grew up, was where the jobs were because of such companies as Digital Equipment Corporation and Data General.

Already in my career I knew that I wanted to work with smaller computers. One has more control. For one, software development is much quicker on your own dedicated machine than on a large mainframe where you submitted your deck of cards and had to wait hours for an assemble or compile. Also, with a smaller computer you are working closer to the hardware and most likely have access to all the operating system software. You don't have to rely on, or work around, software over which you have no control. I guess I'm somewhat of a control freak when it comes to software development.

I landed a job with a startup company that was building a new minicomputer. Wilkinson Computer Sciences was started by a Canadian, Mac Wilkinson. His 16-bit computer, the WCS-881, was more advanced than DEC's PDP-8, which, introduced in 1965, was the most popular minicomputer on the market at the time. Mac's machine was closer in capability to the PDP-11, which had not yet appeared. When I started, the system was in the early stages of development. I remember working on the assembler.

Mac was looking for a market and he found one. He sold his company to Foto-Mem Inc., a company that was in the early stages of developing a mass memory optical storage device based on microfiche cards. They needed a minicomputer to control this mass memory system. I became an employee of Foto-Mem.

There were five of us in the software development group at Foto-Mem. That is where I met my first 'eccentric' programmer, Chris W. He would come to work in his Brooks Brother's suit and penny loafers, hair down to his shoulders, with a briefcase in each hand. He also had two trash cans by his desk, one for 'definite' trash and the other for 'probable' trash. I never got to see any of his finished products at Foto-Mem, but I knew he was special, bordering on genius.

Someone sold the minicomputer as a standalone system to be used at the Raynham Dog Track, south of Boston. It would be a while before they could deliver their first mass memory product so they were happy to make money in any way they could. At the dog track, the computer would be used to compute all the payoffs at the end of a race given the $2 payoffs for win, place and show. It would then display the results on monitors at the cashier's windows. Prior to that, the payoffs would be read off the tote board, quickly written down on a piece of paper, and placed in front of a TV camera which would cause the payoffs to be displayed on the monitors. Now at the end of a race, the system operator would be told the $2 payoffs and simply enter the three payoff amounts (win, place and show) into the computer via the console keyboard which then caused all payoff information (2$, 5$, 10$, etc payoffs) to be displayed on the monitors.

I was elected to implement the system. I wrote the system in assembler language and debugged the hell out of it. The customer decided he wanted me to be the operator for the first week of operation. If anything went wrong, he wanted me there! I wonder what he would have done if a bug had caused the payoffs to be wrong. (I had the feeling that he had one foot in the underworld.) Fortunately, the system worked flawlessly. There was never a bug found in the software. Eventually, after I left Foto-Mem, they were able to electronically read the $2 payoffs and eliminate the human element.

What did I learn from this project? Extreme debugging and testing pays off. I also learned that I shouldn't gamble. After being relieved of my 'operator' duties one day, I decided to bet on a race. I watched as the dogs came up to the starting gate. One seemed particularly energetic and full of life. I bet on him. He won. I went to the cashier's window only to realize that I had given them the number for another dog when I placed my bet. I haven't been to the races since.

Foto-Mem was having financial problems. They hadn't yet sold any of their large systems. They had a layoff. At that time two of the programmers were working on yet-to-be-delivered software for their mass memory product. That left Chris W. and me. I was let go. I didn't think it was right that they let go the only programmer who had so far contributed to the bottom line of the company. However, I could understand it. Chris was a senior programmer and a real find that the company did not want to lose. That was the only time in my 35 years in the industry that I was asked to leave a company.

The photo on the back cover of this book is from a marketing brochure for Mac Wilkinson's mini-computer before his company was bought by Foto-mem.

Chapter 4

Another Canadian Connection

It didn't take long before I got a job with a Canadian company, Consolidated Computer. They were based in Toronto but had a sales and support office in Waltham, a suburb of Boston. The company was one of the first to develop a shared-key-to-disk data entry system that was meant to replace keypunch machines and key-to-tape systems. One minicomputer (PDP-8) could support up to 32 data entry terminals. Data would be entered, edited, stored on disk, and 'peeled' to magnetic tape. The tape could then be read into the mainframe computer for processing. Their product, the Key-Edit 100/85 used 'blind' terminals. They had a full keyboard, but no display. Rather, they had rows of lights that would display status information such as current record, field and column. The operating system was highly interrupt driven with, I believe, 15 levels of interrupt. Keyboard entry was at the highest interrupt level so as not to lose keystrokes. Disk and tape-done interrupts were in there somewhere. I can't remember or even imagine what the other interrupt levels were used for. It was a complex little operating system.

My job at Consolidated was to handle software modifications to the system requested by customers in the states. One of the advantages of a minicomputer based key-to-disk data entry system is that as the data is entered it can be verified and massaged before being written to tape, providing the destination mainframe with cleaner, more error-free data. Examples are 'batch balancing' and 'cross field checks'. Batch balancing allows for a field in each record in a file to be added into an accumulator and at the end of the file, or batch, a total is entered by the operator that must match the accumulated total. A cross-field check might be something like 'field 1 times field 2 should equal field 3'.

A lot of sales were made based on making such requested modifications to the system. I would attempt to make the modification in a general way (i.e. parameter driven) that could be used by more than just the requesting customer. Modifications were also made in coordination with the software group in Toronto and became part of the mother system. Plenty of work was coming in so we hired a second programmer to join the group. After a while the two of us couldn't handle all the work. A request came in for a non-standard batch balancing type check (most requests were for non-standard type checks). At this time Chris W. was no longer working at Foto-Mem so I hired him to implement this new modification on a contract basis. Chris came up with the idea of implementing a very general batch balancing feature. The user could enter a small batch balancing 'program' at the system console (teletype). The program consisted of commands such as "ADD <field #> TO <accumulator #> and "IF <accumulator #> NE <field #>, DISPLAY ERROR". I sold this idea to the company and we were on our way.

It turned out that Chris was somewhat unreliable. He was a hard guy to get a hold of. I later found out that Chris lived a 30-hour day – 20 hours awake, 10 hours asleep. The project deadline was coming and Chris wasn't making much progress. We decided to bring him to Toronto and hold him hostage until he completed the project. I went along to babysit. We put him up at the King Edward Sheraton and kept him in M&Ms until he got the job done. The new feature worked great. And it was the prettiest, best-documented code (assembler language) I had ever seen. All the columns (code, comments) were lined up perfectly. Most lines had a (useful) comment and there were plenty of paragraph comments preceding chunks of code. Chris was a perfectionist. We never found any bugs in his code.

It was at Consolidated that I found out that one of the things in a salesman's toolbox was prevarication. I was on a customer call with the president of our subsidiary somewhere in Connecticut. While in a meeting with the customer, the president was making up stories as to the capabilities of our system. I couldn't believe it. On our drive home I naively scolded him, after which he put me in my place. You don't scold the president no matter how colossal his fabrications.

Not long after that the Canadians asked me to go spend a month in London training a new manager on our system. My stay in Berlin left me with a strong sense of adventure and interest in different countries and cultures. I spent a month in London, saw some great plays, fell in love with a local (I'm a sucker for an accent), and when I returned I asked to be transferred to the company's London office. The transfer was approved by the home office in Canada, but the president of our subsidiary wouldn't allow it because he didn't want to lose the expertise and half of his software development team. Understandable.

During my short stay in Consolidated's London office, I couldn't help but observe some differences between the British and American work environments. For one, there seemed to be this chasm between management and labor, and this was in the software engineering department. A throwback of the class system I suppose. Managers had lots of bennies (benefits) that their individual contributor counterparts did not have. A big one was a company car. At that time it was very expensive to own and maintain a car in Great Britain. I met several Consolidated employees from the Great Britain office who managed to transfer to the head office in Toronto. The first thing they did in Canada was to buy a car. One in particular fulfilled his dream of buying a 1966 Ford Mustang.

One evening, while I was still working at Consolidated, I drove my new German VW into Kenmore Square, Boston. There were several colleges nearby and lots of places to drink and meet women. I made the mistake of parking again on Newbury Street, the same street from where my MGA was stolen almost five years earlier. When I returned to the VW, it was still there, but some of the glass in the wing window was missing. Well, they didn't take much, but I'd never park on Newbury Street again.

After having had my transfer request to the U.K. turned down, I decided to leave Consolidated Computer. I wanted to find work in a more development-oriented company. Consolidated was a sales support group with the major product decisions being made in Canada.

Chapter 5

Harry, Barry and Dave

The experience I gained at Consolidated landed me a job with a local company, which was a competitor of Consolidated, Entrex Inc. (Entry King). Unlike Consolidated, Entrex's development and manufacturing was done locally in Burlington. The company was started by three 26-year old MIT grad student dropouts: Dave Barber, Harry Vickers, and Barry Harder. Barber ran the software group, Vickers hardware, and Harder was president due to his previous experience founding a computer dating service while an undergrad at UC Berkeley. The three were affectionately known by their employees as Harry, Barry and Dave. There were about seven or eight of us in the software development group.

There were many differences between Entrex's System-480 data entry system and Consolidated's Key-Edit system. For one, the System-480 had a real 480 character CRT monitor. Another major difference was the structure of the operating system. Where Key-Edit had 15 levels of interrupt, System-480 had just one level – disk-done. I was in awe of the design of both the hardware and software. How simple and yet powerful it was. One interrupt and it could keep up with 32 data entry operators typing away as fast as they could. And all the while verification checks were being done during data entry. How was this possible? First was how the keystrokes were captured. They were captured entirely by hardware. Each operator's keystrokes were put into a hardware fifo (first in, first out) buffer. Periodically the software would poll the hardware buffers and move keystrokes to a software fifo associated with that terminal's Task Control Block (TCB). The hardware fifos were large enough so that if the software were to temporarily get behind, buffered keystrokes would not be lost.

The operating system was 'event driven' as opposed to 'interrupt driven'. The heart of the operating system was simple. Each terminal (TCB) was serviced in a round-robin fashion. The magnetic tape was also serviced. Whenever a natural pause occurred while servicing a terminal (i.e. disk I/O wait), the operating system would 'PASS' (context switch) to service the next terminal. In the case of some tasks that were compute intensive, PASSes were inserted at strategic points in the code so as not to hog time. I learned that the hard way. I implemented a batch balancing feature. When the batch was finished and the operator entered the pre-calculated total, the software would go through the file and add the specified field in each record to an accumulator and when done would compare the computed total with the expected total. I noticed that the system (all operator's terminals) would hang for short periods of time during the batch balancing process. My batch balancing was hogging compute time. I simply had to add a PASS after adding each field to the accumulator and the problem went away.

During that period in time, a single computer sharing its resources among multiple tasks or users was called 'time sharing' (now referred to as 'multitasking'). One method of time sharing was hardware 'timeslicing'. Each terminal or task was given a specific amount of time (a time slice) that could be given up either voluntarily or via a hardware interrupt if the time limit were up. Interrupts need interrupt service routines that must do things like save registers and current states. That means overhead - overhead which the Entrex system did not have. *Just because a computer provides lots of hardware capabilities such as multi-level interrupts, does not mean the software must use them to be most efficient.*

The system was implemented on a Data General Nova 16-bit mini with 64K bytes of memory. How could it handle so many data entry terminals with such little memory? Memory was broken down into 256-byte chunks or blocks. A block could contain code or data. All code in the system was re-entrant which meant all code could be shared. Multiple terminals could be simultaneously using the same block of code. Data could be shared as well. For example, one data entry operator could be entering a record while a second operator right behind her could be verifying the same record in memory. Any information that was specific to a particular terminal, such as a pointer to the current character in the current record in memory, was kept in that terminal's TCB. One of the original visionary programmers in the group, Gene Kwasniewski, had studied/worked on advanced operating system techniques at MIT (the Multics Operating System I believe) and it showed. The operating system was simple yet sophisticated.

After working on the Entrex system, whenever I would use an operating system capable of performing multiple tasks at one time (i.e. Windows), I would get frustrated if there were any long delays or pauses because I know that the underlying core operating system software could be better. Bill Gates, who I admire greatly, has a lot of strengths (i.e. business acumen, visionary), but designing and implementing the core of an operating system is apparently not one of them.

It was at Entrex that I learned the expression sometimes applied to software: KISS (Keep It Simple Stupid). The concepts I learned working on the Entrex system helped me to design and implement many of the successful systems I worked on throughout my career.

We finished 'Release 6' of the product and got it to market and it was a success. We then started focusing on features for the next release of the product. As with most companies, the goal was to keep coming out with incremental software releases within a relatively short period of time. I had been mostly working on data entry verification check features. My thoughts went back to Consolidated Computer and Chris W's implementation of the batch balancing feature. I took that concept further and expanded it into an end user language like COBOL or BASIC where the user could implement his own field, record and batch-end checks. This would eliminate all parameter driven edit checks such as cross-footing, range checking and batch balancing and give complete control and more importantly, flexibility, to the user. For example, instead of having lower and upper range check parameters assigned to a field, the program statement to accomplish this task would look like: "IF <field #> LT <lower range> OR <field #> GT <upper range>, PAUSE "Field out of range".

Other members of the software group liked the idea and they took it a step further. The language would be used to allow the user flexibility in formatting the output tape, again eliminating some of the parameter-driven options that currently existed. The problem with this idea was that it was a major change to the system that would take lots longer than an incremental release. Fortunately, Entrex was still a very engineering oriented company and they decided to go ahead with the major system rewrite. They were willing to take a chance and hopefully not lose market share due to a long pause in releasing new features. Most companies would not take this kind of risk.

The first thing I did was to attend a seminar on building compilers. I decided to build an 'interpretive' compiler. User programs would be compiled into interpretive tables (i.e. op code, operand, operand), which would work well with our virtual memory scheme (256-byte blocks). A run time interpreter or executor would execute the command tables. Again, the interpreter and command tables were re-entrant so could be simultaneously shared by multiple terminals. Before starting detailed design and implementation, I brought in Chris W. to critique my design.

We went ahead and implemented 'Release 7' and it was a major success. There wasn't another data entry system in the world that could touch it. The combination of the super efficient (and bulletproof) operating system and the end user flexibility was unbeatable. As a result, a German company, Nixdorf Computer AG, signed a contract to OEM the Entrex system throughout Europe and other parts of the world.

I consider my contribution to Entrex as the most significant of my career. I felt my contribution played a major role in the financial success of the company. The reason Nixdorf, and I assume other customers, were so interested in the system is because of the flexibility allowed by the end user programmability. Of course, I have to thank Chris W. for the original idea, which I just expanded upon, and for the management at Entrex who were brave enough to go ahead with the implementation.

It certainly was more enjoyable working for an engineering oriented company as opposed to one that is more sales oriented, as was Consolidated Computer in Waltham. It was good to work for people who better understood the software development process. One engineer who I shared an office with at Entrex, our resident Mafia connection, Dick Priori, nickname Guido, told me that at his previous company, in an effort to boost productivity and meet deadlines, programmers were paid 50 cents for each assembly language instruction they produced. Data structures (i.e. diagnostic messages) also counted. Hard to believe, but this is a true story. As you would expect, the result was a very bloated system with lots of very verbose messages. After learning the error of their ways, they paid the programmers 50 cents for each instruction or memory location they eliminated.

We worked hard at Entrex and we played hard. Friday evenings we would often unwind together at the local HoJo's (Howard Johnsons) with a bunch of beers. On occasion we would go to lunch at a popular restaurant in the next town over, Billerica. The Everglades was an institution, renowned for it's Italian style pizza pie and other favorites such as fried clams. When I was a kid my dad would drive us the 20 miles just to eat their pizza and clams. If we got to a third round of beers, then we were there for the rest of the day and part of the evening (the Entrex crowd, not my family!). Unfortunately The Everglades no longer exists.

I left Entrex after only a year, but not because I didn't enjoy working there. I was offered a Job in Costa Rica, and having been in Central America several times while at NSA, and still having a strong desire to experience living in other countries, it was an offer I couldn't turn down. I regretted leaving the folks at Entrex. I learned a lot from them and considered them all good friends. But this is not the end of my relationship with Entrex. I will eventually come back to the states and get to work with these good people again.

Oh. While at Entrex, I was sent to England on a business trip to troubleshoot some software problems at a client site. While there I connected up with the woman I previously fell in love with while working with Consolidated. Time changes things. If Consolidated had transferred me when I requested, I probably would have married her.

The photo on the front cover of this book is from the front cover of an Entrex marketing brochure (K.I.S.S. text added by me), the message being that the system is extremely easy to use ("And because it's so simple to operate, you can hire the operators on looks alone").

Chapter 6

Off to the Jungle

My co-worker at Consolidated Computer had left and went to work for a small company that was building a time-sharing small business system with a dictionary/hash-file based database. Applications included inventory control, accounts receivable and payable. The hardware was comprised of a Data General mini, multi-platter disk, system console, printer, and multiple user CRT terminals. All was written in assembler language. The owner of this small company sold the system to an American living in San Jose, Costa Rica who started a small computer company together with a couple of Costa Ricans. The system required some major modifications in both the operating system and the applications.

The American partner of the Costa Rican company offered my ex co-worker a job but she wasn't interested in going to Costa Rica. She told me about it and after an interview over a few beers, I got the job. We rented an office in Waltham where I got the software up and running on some newly purchased hardware. The code was a mess. One of the first things I did was to rip out the time-sharing operating system and replace it with an Entrex-like event-driven operating system. A major change to the concept of the system was that in Costa Rica, the terminals would be in remote locations communicating with the mini over dial-up asynchronous communications links. Remote printers were also supported. This was 1972, years before the advent of PC's and Hayes modems. This system was the first of its kind in Costa Rica. I eventually brought another Entrex programmer down into the 'jungle' to help out with the software. As the applications were written in assembler language, there was always plenty to do. The core operating system did its job with no problems. Multiple customers had remote terminals and printers in their offices running their business applications on the computer in our office.

Before leaving for Costa Rica my boss-to-be suggested I bring a vehicle with me, and he recommended a Land Rover, as that was the most popular vehicle at the time in the country. I found and bought a used pale green Land Rover with a black soft top. My first (and only) 4-wheel drive vehicle. I felt I needed to practice using it off road. One evening after having a few at HoJo's we went over a friends house (Guido) to have something to eat. His house backed up to a wooded area. In I went. The next day I had to return to pick up the Land Rover after an enormous vehicle with a crane extracted it from the woods. It was now leaking transmission fluid.

My first night in Costa Rica was spent on my boss' couch. I was excited about being there and couldn't sleep. I kept hearing the clip clop of horse's hoofs throughout the night. I found out later that the horseman was the local neighborhood security guard. Each neighbor paid a small fee each month for the guard to keep an eye on their property. I moved into the same neighborhood but unfortunately the horseman, who was very old, retired and was replaced by a younger guard who did his rounds on a motorcycle.

Costa Rica was a great place to live. Weather in the central plateau, where the bulk of the population lives, was great. There was no need for either heating or air conditioning. Costa Ricans liked Americans. There was a lot of crime, but mostly non-violent, non-confrontational, theft. The police used to carry screwdrivers instead of guns. For parking violations, they would remove the license plate of the offending vehicle and the owner would have to go to the police station and pay a fine to get it back. That was the only way they could get someone to pay a parking fine.

When my Land Rover arrived I had to take a train out to the port of Limon, which was located on the Atlantic side of Costa Rica, to pick it up. Coming back was a long drive, lots of it over dirt roads and through banana plantations. I remember having to stop once behind several cars stopped in the middle of the road. Several people were standing around while watching a 3-toed sloth cross the road. The drive was brutal and wasn't helped by the low gear ratio of the Land Rover. It didn't take long before I decided it really wasn't the right vehicle for me in Costa Rica. For one, all other Land Rovers there had hard tops. Mine could easily be broken into. I was surprised that for the few months that I had it there, the floor and seat mats weren't stolen. I traded the Land Rover for a maroon VW bug. One really didn't need a 4-wheel drive vehicle in Costa Rica, although the roads then, and now, are full of potholes so having a vehicle with a robust suspension is a good thing.

I met my true love in Costa Rica. I had been dating Costa Rican women for the first six months there. Then I met a Brit one evening in a bar and we became friends and would go out together to meet women. One evening we met a couple of woman at one of San Jose's large dance halls where they had live Latin music. We made a date to meet them at an English Pub in the heart of downtown a few days later. Tony, my British friend, arrived there first. Apparently, the two women sent two substitutes in their place. Tony called me and said he couldn't do that to me. He wouldn't wish these two (women?) on anyone. I was to come to the pub, but I was going to be become George. Ralph would not show up.

Tony also brought with him that evening a 19-year old German woman who, for something to do while she was on a 6-month vacation before college, started cleaning Tony's apartment. Tony had a young, very good-looking Costa Rican maid, who apparently didn't get much cleaning done when she was there. Tony had mentioned me to the German woman, Barbara, but she wasn't interested because I was 12 years older than she. She came with Tony that evening and was set up to meet a 25-year old Costa Rican. When I arrived, as George, all were there. It didn't take long for Barbara and me to decide to leave the group and head to a discothèque for a night of dancing and conversation. Our romance started.

After dancing and romancing one evening, we decided to take a trip in my maroon VW to one of the areas big Volcanoes, Poas. Adjacent to Poas was a beautiful lagoon. It was about 2 a.m. We would arrive around dawn. It would be a nice and quiet time to be there and experience the beauty of it all. Driving in Costa Rica was always a challenge due to the lack of road signs. We were driving through the city of Heredia, were lost, spotted a policeman and stopped to ask him which road to take for Poas. He smiled and pointed to the road we should take. As we entered the road we realized he was sending us up a one-way road in the wrong direction. But that was Costa Rica. After that evening the VW was named "Poas".

Barbara was planning to major in math and computer science in college. She had already done some programming. I convinced the owners of our company to let me hire her. They of course thought I wanted to hire her only so that I could be close to her every day. I suppose there was some truth in that, but we really could use the help and she was a really good programmer. We tore out the math routines in the system, which I didn't trust, and she implemented very efficient, reliable, bit-shifting quadruple precision math routines. She earned her meager Costa Rican-scale pay and then some.

One day when Barbara and I left the office and approached Poas, we noticed that there was glass missing from the wing window, replaced in part by some fresh blood. Someone got our neat denim and corduroy jackets. But that was Costa Rica.

Costa Rica has changed a lot since I've lived there. The police now carry guns. San Jose, the capitol, is a lot more crowded with much more traffic congestion. When I was there about five years ago, I was sitting in traffic in one of the main streets in the downtown area and two locals got out of their cars and started swinging fists at each other in the middle of the street. There is lots more violent crime there nowadays. Banks and busses are being robbed by masked gunmen carrying AK47s. Columbians trafficking their drugs. Lots more homes protected by bars and razer-sharp concertina wire. But it is still a great place to live. One just has to get away from San Jose. The Ticos, as they are affectionately called, are still very friendly people and they still like us **North** Americans (they are Americans as well). They are called Ticos because of their habit of adding the suffix "tico" to words to make them even more diminutive than they are. For example, poquito (a little bit) becomes poquitico (a very little bit) and chiquito (small) becomes chiquitico. If you're referring to just females, they are Ticas.

Some things haven't changed in Costa Rica. For one, the roads are still bad. But with all its failings, it's still a popular retirement destination. The largest minority in Costa Rica is North Americans, comprising about 4% of the population. Cheap, quality healthcare is available. On my last trip there I made sure I took care of all my then current dental needs.

How was working in Costa Rica different than working in the states? We were a small company, with my boss being an American, so I don't remember there being lots of differences. One difference we used to joke about is scheduling meetings. When setting a time for a meeting, we would ask "Is that Costa Rican time or Gringo time?". Costa Rican meetings would start 20 or more minutes after the scheduled time. Labor was cheap in Costa Rica. We had a go-for who would go out and pick us up some sandwiches for lunch on busy days. We were there during the gas shortage, experienced both in Costa Rica and the states, where everyone had to wait in long lines for a few gallons of gasoline. Our go-for would spend the day waiting in lines, gassing up our cars. Another result of cheap labor was that many middle-class Costa Ricans had live-in maids. Many homes and even apartments (like my 2-bedroom apartment) had maid's quarters. In those days the maids were women coming from the farms in the rural parts of Costa Rica. Today they are Nicaraguan immigrants looking for a better life.

When offered the opportunity to live and work in Costa Rica, I jumped at the chance. After spending a month in Panama for NSA, I knew I liked the Latin lifestyle. I wouldn't want to live in Panama, but after reading up on Costa Rica, it was an easy decision to move there. One day while driving in downtown San Jose, I saw a familiar gringo face walking across the street. He was a civilian working for our government in Panama in the group where I installed the NSA computer system. Apparently, after his tour of duty was up, he and his family were driving back to the states, and they never got any further than Costa Rica.

Chapter 7

Back to Germany, Finally

After I had been a year in Costa Rica, it was time for Barbara to return to Germany and start college. What to do? I certainly wasn't averse to living in Germany. I wrote a letter directly to Heinz Nixdorf, founder of Nixdorf Computer AG. I told him that I was planning to move to Germany with my 'fiancée' and that I had experience working on the Entrex system that his company was currently selling in Europe. They flew me out for an interview that resulted in a job offer. They moved both me and my 'fiancée' to Paderborn, Germany. The Costa Rican company, Sistemas Analiticos, is still around. I was recently in San Jose and had lunch with one of the Costa Rican founders who is now happily retired.

Paderborn is in northern Germany, in the middle of nowhere. It is Heinz Nixdorf's hometown. The computer industry in Germany tended to be more in the larger cities like Frankfurt or Munich. Leaving Nixdorf for another job meant moving to another part of Germany. But Germans are nowhere near as mobile as we are. They may work for one company for their entire lives. They are likely to buy and live in one house for the rest of their lives.

Nixdorf Computer was founded in 1952 and eventually became the fourth largest computer company in Europe specializing in banking systems as well as mini-computer based business systems and point-of-sale systems. And of course they were a major reseller of the Entrex data entry system. Their headquarters was in a square, multistory bronze and glass building on a quiet street in Paderborn. That building is now, according to their website, the largest computer museum in the world. While in Paderborn, I lived in an apartment on the same street. I had a two-minute commute by foot. Heaven.

Most of the people in the software group spoke English, which was good since my German was not very good at the time. Most documentation was in English. One engineer wrote a functional specification for a homegrown floppy disk drive. He wrote it in German and he translated "floppy disk" to the German equivalent "Weiche Platte". Management told him they did not want to invent a new term and he should use the English term. His response was to rewrite the entire spec in English.

Most of the time during my year at Nixdorf was spent working with the Entrex system. I trained several software engineers on the system and I worked closely with marketing to define enhancements to the system specific to Nixdorf's market and coordinate those enhancements with the Entrex software group in Burlington. Oh. My title was "Software Engineer". I had never been called an engineer before. In the states, we were still 'programmers'. An 'engineer' without a college degree … cool.

At one point Nixdorf decided that they could and should build their own data entry system. I was not asked to work on the project but they did call me in one day to describe the inner workings of the Entrex system. I carefully explained to them how it worked, the event driven O/S, the page-oriented virtual memory manager, re-entrant and shareable code and data, the hardware fifos. Well, they ended up designing the operating system after some IBM model where each terminal owned a fixed chunk of memory (i.e. 8K) for both code and data. Needless to say, after many months of development, their prototype could not support even eight simultaneous terminals. Management was irate. I smiled. The project was canceled.

My days at Nixdorf were numbered. They were not going to give me anything meaningful to do. I found out when I quit that the software manager was not happy when he was told that I would be working in his group. I was forced upon him. He was not involved in the interview process. At the interview I met with a high level negotiator, Niels Eskelson, presumably because I had originally written directly to Heinz Nixdorf. In that letter I had suggested that I could work as a consultant rather than an employee and that's why I assume the negotiator was involved. After the interview they decided to offer me a job as an employee.

When joining or leaving a company, it is a German tradition to have an "Einstand" (first day) or "Ausstand" (going-away) party. I didn't know about that when I joined, but when I left I threw an Ausstand party. What's different about a German going-away party than one in the states is that the leaving employee is responsible for paying for the party (treating all those who attend). I made a lot of good friends at Nixdorf. While working at Nixdorf, I married my sweetheart in her hometown in southern Germany.

Chapter 8

First Contract Programming Experience

I spent the summer of 1975 in my wife's hometown. While there, I took an intensive German language course and really improved my German. After the summer we decided to move to the Frankfurt area. She wanted to attend Darmstadt University, which had a good Computer Science program. One of her instructors there at the time was David Parnas, a pioneer in software engineering credited with developing the concept of modular program design which is the foundation of today's object oriented programming. It was a good area for me to look for work. We rented a small, furnished apartment in Darmstadt until I had a job and knew where I'd be working.

I answered an ad I found in one of the Frankfurt newspapers. A small company (the owner/salesman and a secretary) was looking for a programmer to implement some billing software on a minicomputer. Selling computers was new to Herr Griese, but I got the impression that he had been reasonably successful at selling business machines including typewriters. He drove an early seventies 200-series Mercedes sedan, which was not a limo but was a stretched version. (One of the most beautiful cars on earth in my opinion is a late sixties, early seventies Mercedes 200-series cabriolet/convertible). It had a car phone, which was not at all common in those days. Computer software was something he was just learning about.

Herr Griese hired me to implement a billing system on a General Automation 16-bit mini with a 10MB disk and 64KB of memory (The T.O.M. System). The user terminal was a 512 character CRT. The system could support up to four terminals. The operating software was a commercial version of Fortran with an ISAM (Index Sequential Access Method) file system. Commercial version of Fortran – strange. I agreed to do the project on a fixed-price basis (10,000DM if I remember correctly). The project took several months. While implementing the software, I kept running into one major problem. At the end of the billing cycle, the process of computing all the bills included a number of steps of record and file banging and updating. Often during this process, the system would crash. It would crash during different, random steps of the process so it was impossible to figure out what was happening. And of course I had no control whatsoever over the operating software. (Argh!) I couldn't troubleshoot the problem at that level. I ended up putting checkpoints or restart points into the software, so that the update process could be restarted and would continue from where it left off. What a crock. But it worked.

When I delivered the final product, Herr Griese told me that I would get paid when the customer paid him. I told him, in German, and in no uncertain terms, that that's not the way it works. The results of my recent German lessons were kicking in. I got paid.

Chapter 9

The London Connection

A short time later, I interviewed with a company that was marketing intelligent terminals (CRT monitor, Intel 8008 microprocessor, 7" floppy disk, printer, synchronous and asynchronous communications capabilities). I was very interested because, as I've mentioned, I like 'small'. Control, control, control. They were very interested in me but didn't have the authority at the time to hire a new engineer. They were interviewing for a future position. They were a subsidiary of a London-based company, Interscan. I couldn't wait for them and kept interviewing and was hired by Battelle Institute in Frankfurt

I don't remember much about my two weeks with Battelle except that I got the impression that not much work got done there. Reminded me of the NSA employee who could spend a whole day socializing and not getting any work done. Interscan called and said the position opened up and they were ready for me. Battelle wasn't really a good fit for me (unless I couldn't find anything else), so I gave my notice at Battelle after which they immediately escorted me to the door.

Interscan was located in Moerfelden, a small city just outside of Frankfurt. We were lucky and found an unfurnished apartment there. I had a 3-minute commute by car. Moerfelden was also close to Darmstadt University.

I ended up doing more work for the British office of Interscan. For the Ontel intelligent terminal, I implemented a stand-alone word processor. It was primitive by today's standards, but it was one of the first on the market. A follow-on project involved integrating the word processing software with their mini-based data processing/entry system. Documents were stored on the mini but entered and modified, a page at a time, on the Ontel terminal. While working at Interscan, I spent a good deal of time in the London area. The main office was in Hounslow near Heathrow, but I remember spending a lot of time debugging in a neat old brick building in Ealing.

At one point, I had my car in England and my wife came over and we drove up through Lake Country into Scotland. One of the highlights of that trip was eating a Nessie Burger gotten from a vending truck parked next to Loch Ness. Another was when a German driver forgot he was supposed to be driving on the left and nearly hit us head on. It's easy to forget when you're driving on a country road with no other cars in sight. In Inverness, Scotland we spent a night in a stone mansion that had been turned into a Bed and Breakfast. Before dinner we were asked to come down to the guest living room and meet the other guests and have a drink. We then went into the guest dining room and sat at a long table with other guests and enjoyed our meal. All of this felt like it was right out of an Agatha Christie novel. During that trip, we also stayed in a Bed & Breakfast in the very picturesque Scottish seaside village of "Algol" (the computer language, "ALGOrithmic Language", designed to fix some of the inherent problems with FORTRAN).

My projects in England came to an end. The German subsidiary was having financial problems and it appeared that the end was in sight. I had now been living in Germany for two and a half years. There just wasn't much work in all of Germany for 'systems' programmers (software engineers). Most was at the applications level. So I convinced my wife that it was time to go to the states. She hadn't completed her degree, but she had the equivalent of an American bachelors degree. A German degree is equivalent to our masters.

I called Entrex and was offered a job immediately. Tom Genova, a co-worker when I worked at Entrex, was now head of the software group. Before heading to the states, my wife and I spent some down time in her hometown. A few days before my flight to the states, Tom called and told me that he had some bad news. "Nixdorf has just acquired us". He asked me if I still wanted the job. I did. After arriving in the states, my wife had no problem finding a job as a software engineer working on network software.

Part of the fun of living and working in another country is experiencing the cultural differences. A couple of differences stand out for me. In German, as in many languages, there are two different forms of the personal pronouns. For example, in German there is "Sie" formal and "du", informal for the word "you". There are rules when to use each form. For example, when speaking to a stranger, one would use "Sie" and when speaking to a child, one would use "du". The question becomes, when does one start using "du" when getting to know someone. Well, one woman I worked with in Moerfelden told me that she used the Sie form to keep some of the people she worked with at arms length. I guess she liked me because she would use the "du" form with me. Being American, and not really worrying too much about the proper protocol, I would usually simply use the "du" form with younger people and out of respect would use the "Sie" form with older people until they used the "du" form with me.

While working at Nixdorf in Paderborn I noticed how important titles were to Germans. Mr. Fetzer, or Herr Fetzer in German, had his doctorate and employees had to address him as Herr Doktor Fetzer. Life in America is so much simpler. This reminds me of a related incident that occurred towards the end of my career. I was working in a large software group with many imported engineers from India and China. There was some sort of issue being hotly debated via a flurry of emails. One import signed his email as "Doctor SoAndSo", possibly hoping it would add to the credibility of his views. This is something Americans don't normally do. Anyway, he got a number of responses from engineers asking his advice for their medical problems. After all, he was a doctor.

Chapter 10

Back to My Friends at Entrex

Nixdorf-Entrex was lots bigger this time around. Success allowed them to grow. They were looking for new markets to conquer. Someone came up with the idea of building a geographically distributed data processing system, which of course would also have strong data entry capabilities. A database could be distributed throughout a country but the fact that there would be multiple geographically distributed databases would be transparent. It would look like one database and would be tied together over an X.25 network. This was in the late seventies and the Internet was nowhere in sight, but public X.25 networks were springing up. The system would have the Entrex event driven O/S, an ISAM (Index Sequential Access Method) database, a high level language for the development of applications, assorted I/O drivers (i.e. printer, tape), and all the network layers as defined in the X.25 implementation standards. I was elected project leader and had, at times, up to six additional software engineers in the group. The product/project was named "Nomad" (Network Oriented Method for Accessing Data).

Interesting to note that only half of the programmers in the group had degrees in Computer Science. It was the late seventies and it was still possible to become a programmer without a degree in Computer Science or without a degree at all.

By now Entrex had improved its data entry system with more data processing and communications capabilities.

Because of communications, the system now had more than one level of interrupt. They also had a separate shared-key-to-disk word processing system. So Nomad was just one of several projects/groups within the software department. There was no pressure to get Nomad quickly up and running as there were no customers waiting on the product. We were allowed to take our time and do it right. As a group we developed detailed functional specs (how it looks to the user) and implementation specs. It was truly a group effort. We also came up with detailed coding standards. This would be the best-documented system ever! Unfortunately, there were not yet higher-level languages commonly used for the implementation of systems software so all would be done in assembler language. And all code would be new code, taking concepts and ideas from the existing Entrex systems. We were still using Data General 16-bit minis. Once all specs were approved, we were on our way. We worked hard, and at the end of the week we continued the ritual of de-stressing at HoJo's. They were fun times.

As time went on, Nixdorf started making itself felt within their Entrex subsidiary. They replaced the VP of Engineering with their own man (an American). He was not a great fan of the Nomad project. His expertise was building computers and he convinced headquarters in Germany to let us build a new 32-bit computer. This is the first time in my career, but not the last, when I felt someone in the company was doing something more for his own personal gain than for the good of the company. Sure would look good on his resume.

Nomad development and Friday night beers continued. Eventually we got a new company president. We were on schedule and close to having Nomad ready for market. We were months away. Then one day they lowered the boom and canceled Nomad. The reason they gave was that it competed with a product being developed in Germany. (I wonder if it was as good as their attempt to build a data entry system). I guess stuff like this happens when one company buys out another. Another reason I heard, which was probably true, was that Nomad was a product without a market. That Friday night we had a Nomad wake at HoJo's.

Nomad was my first experience at managing people. I think I did a pretty good job. However, one reason is because of the quality of the people in the group. There were a couple of engineers in the group whose egos were commensurate with their talent. More than once I had to act as referee during design meetings. At one of the meetings, I was told by one of the engineers to go f..k myself. If this guy weren't as good as he was, he would have been out the door in a minute. He was an excellent implementer and worth taking some major s..t from. The first piece of code he wrote for the company was an HDLC communications protocol trace program. HDLC frames were output to a terminal for debug purposes.

The trace facility was written in assembly language and was broken up into 256-byte blocks in order to work with our virtual memory management system. The code spanned about seven blocks. The first time the code was built into the system, it worked, without one bug. Zero machine debug time was required. This engineer's style was to extensively desk debug his code before it was entered into the system (we did not have workstations at that time and all code was entered into the system by data entry operators). Later on I realized one of the reasons that this particular engineer was so good at producing bug-free code. I once watched him at the debug terminal (his code wasn't always bug-free). He was all fingers, both literally and figuratively. This was just not one of his strengths. So he made up for it by producing mostly error-free code.

This might be a good time to talk about coding styles or habits. Some engineers will spend more time up front during the coding process, needing less time for debug. And vice versa. There are engineers at both ends of the spectrum, like the one just mentioned, and engineers at all points in between. Some people simply enjoy debugging more than coding, and vice versa. Whether one extreme is more productive than the other may depend upon the development environment – the coding process and the quality of the debug tools. If the debugging tools are poor, it makes sense to do more desk debugging. Usually, though, those who spend more time up front produce better code.

More important than the coding/debugging ratio, however, is the amount of time spent designing versus implementing. Poor, or a lack of, adequate design can lead to serious logic errors (as opposed to simple coding errors). Logic errors may not be easy to fix, depending on their severity. Forgetting to check for buffer overflow is an easy problem to fix, but something more serious like underestimating the resources needed to perform a particular task (i.e. memory or cpu time) could be serious and require major code changes. More time spent during the design phase means less time spent during the other implementation phases, especially during the maintenance phase.

In regards to the design and implementation of a piece of software, there's something I've really never understood or agreed with, and that is having one person design a piece of software, and having someone else implement it. I've met very few programmers who would want to implement someone else's design. Shortly after I started working the first time for Entrex, I was to implement a field range check feature. A senior engineer came up with a design of the feature that I thought made it awkward for the user to specify. I came up with another way of doing it, which I felt was more user-friendly. The head of the software group decided that I should implement the feature as defined by the senior engineer. I wasn't happy about his decision but implemented the flawed design. Fortunately, that engineer left the company and the edit check was thrown out when replaced by the flexible user language implemented in release 7 of the product as described earlier.

Obviously however, some engineers have better design skills than others. And sometimes you have to convince an engineer to sign-up to implement someone else's design. Here's how we handled this during the Nomad design phase. First, the system was broken down into pieces (i.e. O/S, user language, distributed File Management System, communications software, device drivers, etc). Each piece was assigned to an engineer who had design responsibility for his or her piece. We held design review meetings for each piece. During the review process, each engineer could point out flaws or suggest improvements in another engineer's design. The determining factor would be the consensus of all engineers in the group. It was a very democratic process. Since the designer-owner had spent more time and thought on his or her piece, his or her vote counted more and others had to convince the owner of the benefits of change. And of course in the case of deadlock, there was always the project leader, but I don't remember it getting to that point very often. We had some egos in our group, but all were fairly reasonable people.

For those pieces in the system that interfaced with the end user or customer, there were two types of design specs – functional and implementation. The functional spec described exactly how the feature (or product) would look to the user. It resembled a user's guide. (In smaller companies where I worked, where there was no tech-writing team, it *was* the user's guide.) It was a description of the feature (or product) that would be reviewed by and signed off by all interested groups within the company. All pieces would also have an implementation spec that described *how* the software for this feature would be implemented. For example, the language's functional spec described the language syntax and things like how to create and execute user programs. The language's implementation spec spelled out things like how the compiler worked and what the resultant compiled interpretive tables looked like. In the case of pieces that didn't interface with the end user, but rather interfaced with software engineers in the group, the implementation spec contained both how the feature or service was to be implemented and gave a detailed description of the programmer's interface (i.e. inputs and outputs), sometimes referred to as the API (Application Programmer's Interface).

Part of the system design task was to make sure all the pieces fit together in a consistent way providing a consistent view of the system to the user. In the case of Nomad, that responsibility fell to the project leader. In other cases it could fall to one or more lead architects. It would depend on the size of the project. In any case, I feel strongly that architects should also be implementers. They need to be able to architect implementable ideas. And they need to be able to defend their designs within the group.

I happen to have a strong interest in the system/user interface. One of the tasks I enjoyed most was making complex systems appear simple to the end user. The syntax of the language I defined at Entrex was taken from both Cobol and Basic, leaning more towards the verboseness of Cobol. The language was to be used primarily by data entry (former keypunch) supervisors. I had a reputation at Entrex for being really good when it came to user-interface level design, maybe because I'm a liberal arts guy. For a number of years after Entrex, I felt that I was probably up there with the best UI guys in the industry. My bubble was burst however when the Apple Macintosh was introduced with it's user-friendly Graphical User Interface (GUI – pronounced gooey).

Interesting to note that in 1988 Apple filed suit against Microsoft for copying it's GUI in its Windows operating system. The irony of that is that Apple's GUI looked very much like Xerox's graphical user interface. Not to be left out, Xerox filed suit against Apple. Both Apple and Xerox lost their lawsuits.

Thinking back over the years and the many companies that I've worked for, I was fortunate enough to be able to design the user interface for many of the products/systems that I worked on. That included the definition of many of the system's features. Some of the larger companies had people in their product marketing department who would get involved in the product definition. Nixdorf, Germany was one of those companies. Many times someone in sales or marketing would just supply a list of requirements for a system that I would turn into a functional specification/user's guide. In any case, it's a task that needs to be shared among the different departments and who does the most work may depend upon who has the most interest or time.

My management style was emerging during the Nomad days. Simply put, I tried to manage others as I would like to be managed. That meant delegating as much responsibility as a person wanted or could handle. And along with that responsibility came the commensurate authority to make decisions. You can't make someone responsible for something that they don't feel is theirs. As an example, take the range check feature that I implemented at Entrex according to another engineers (crappy) design. I didn't feel responsible if the customer was unhappy with how the feature worked. I did not own that feature. If you own a feature, it has your name on it, and I would hope that you would want it to be the best that it can be.

Note that I said "as much responsibility as a person ... could handle". There are engineers who simply lack good design skills. In that case, I would assign that engineer to a task not requiring lots of design. In the top-down design of a system, the further down you go, the easier the design task is. There are fewer decisions to make. Writing software at the user interface level is lots more complicated than writing software at the hardware level. For one, lots more defensive coding is required at the user interface level. Think of all the ways the user can misuse the system. At the hardware level, all that is required is a soft interface to the hardware, allowing programmers hopefully a simple interface to the hardware (i.e. for a piece of communications equipment, an Open (initialize), Close, Send and Receive interface).

This concept also holds true within the communications layers on a communications link. The physical or hardware layer is the simplest. The link layer is a point-to-point layer responsible for moving data between two points. It's certainly more complicated than the physical layer due to such requirements as guaranteeing delivery of data between the two points. Some sort of error detection and or correction protocol is required. And the higher layers which guarantee delivery of data between two end points over multiple point-to-point links gets even more complicated. Bottom line – when deciding what tasks to assign to which programmers, the skills of those engineers and not just their titles or time in grade should be considered. A junior engineer may have better design skills or a better feel for user-interface programming than a senior engineer. I realize that this may sound very obvious, but I've seen tasks assigned to engineers based solely on their title. The job description for that title says an engineer should be able to perform a particular task. That's just not the way it works. We all have different skill sets. It's up to the manager to determine his/her people's strengths and weaknesses and consider them when planning projects.

I'm just reminded of an incident that happened during my year with Entrex. One of the programmers I worked with had the opinion that when it came to implementing a piece of software, there was only one right way (his way). At some point, he was convinced by me and others that there may be several 'right' ways to implement a piece of software. He was now a manager at Nixdorf-Entrex and was very comfortable with delegating the software design responsibility to the programmers working for him. He went on to have a very successful software management career before starting his own very successful company. Understanding that there may be many right ways to implement a piece of software makes it easier for a manager to delegate that responsibility.

Chapter 11

Plotting Along

The former president of Entrex, Don Feddersen (The Fed), became the president of Applicon, one of the first vendors of CAD/CAM (Computer Aided Design and Manufacturing) systems. Applicon was just a few buildings away from Nixdorf-Entrex in Burlington. It was a few buildings closer to HoJo's.

Dave Barber, one of the founders of Entrex, went to work for Don as VP of Sales and Tom Genova became their VP of Software Engineering. Barbara Purchia, one of the original Entrex software engineers, became a software manager. Others also moved from Nixdorf-Entrex to Applicon. I was one of the last. I went to work for Barbara as the project leader of the plotter software group. Among other tasks, my user-interface skills were tapped to make the system's plotter/user interface more user-friendly.

The work was not very exciting, but it was good to be back with friends in a good working environment. The last weeks and months at Nixdorf-Entrex were rough. Dealing with office politics is just not one of my strengths.

One good thing that happened to me while at Applicon is that my wife gave birth to twin boys. She would take some years off from her career to raise the boys. Up to that point in time, she had a successful career as a software engineer in the networking group at GenRad, a company building and selling automated test equipment. I got to know many of her colleagues as she did mine during parties or Friday nights at HoJos. I still remember vividly the yearly GenRad road rallies. They would start early in the morning and end up at some undisclosed destination, like a state park, for a picnic. On our first road rally we had the distinction of being the last group (two couples in each car) to arrive.

Chapter 12

What, Me, a Manager?

A year after I joined Applicon, I was approached by the former VP of Engineering at Nixdorf-Entrex, Eric Jackson. Eric was now president of Amnet, a company that was building X.25 packet switches, both new hardware and software.

Each packet switch, or network node, was made up of multiple processors, each with it's own set of tasks, communicating with each other via a chunk of shared memory. As I remember it, hardware architecture seemed somewhat complicated, making software communications between processors somewhat awkward and inefficient. Certainly didn't fit the KISS philosophy. In addition to handling all the requisite X.25 communications layers, each node maintained a distributed, replicated database containing network information. It was being implemented in 'C' and assembler. The 'C' language was becoming the standard language for communications software (leaving the other popular high-level language at the time, Pascal, in the dust) although many time critical functions were still written in assembler. Amnet was also supporting some legacy systems (voice response communications systems) that the company sold before Eric took over.

Eric was looking for someone to head up the software department and I had the X.25 knowledge and project management experience. This would be a big change for me. There were four engineers working on the legacy systems and fifteen or so on the X.25 project. At that time there weren't dual-path compensation tracks, management and individual contributor, so moving up into management was the best way to keep pushing the upper salary limits. Could I do it? It was time to find out. My friends at Applicon were not upset when I left. It was all in the family.

As previously mentioned, I had already established a management style during my Nomad days at Nixdorf-Entrex. I managed people as I would like to be managed - delegate. Give people as much responsibility as they can handle or want to handle. Oversee the overall design and implementation of a product/project, making sure all the pieces fit together coherently and that all the project goals were being met.

Unfortunately my management style didn't work well at Amnet. There was no problem with the legacy system support. The work in that group was going just fine. When I joined the company, the X.25 project was already behind schedule. The software design was complete and tasks already assigned to the members of the team. Implementation had already begun. One of the first things that I did was to sit down with each software engineer, understand his assigned task (piece of the system), and determine where he was in terms of his meeting his currently assigned goals (schedule). Then I came up with what I hoped was a realistic schedule with several milestones along the way. From that point on I would periodically poll all the software engineers as to whether they were on schedule or not for the first major milestone. They assured me that they were all on schedule.

I kept busy dealing with design, implementation, personnel and legacy system issues. We also hired several contractors to work on the network node database software. As we got closer to the deadline, it was becoming clear that many of the troops were not on schedule. We went into crunch mode and started working weekends. When the day came to integrate all the 'completed' system parts for the first milestone, it was clear that a number of the engineers weren't ready, some of them far from being ready. How could this happen? They all claimed they were on schedule and assured me that they would meet this deadline. Oooops.

My first failure. I had to ask myself "why". What could I have done differently. I think one of the problems was the lack of experience of some of the engineers. My 'delegate' management style worked well with the Nomad software engineers because most were top-notch, experienced engineers. Some of the less experienced Amnet engineers could have used guidance in implementing their pieces. I didn't recognize that. It would also have been helpful if there were more milestones more often with demonstrable results. Even if some throw-away code had to be implemented in order to test and demo a piece of code, it would be worth the extra amount of time to find out earlier if there were problems with meeting a deadline, or problems implementing a particular design.

Thinking back, if we could have demo'd Nomad earlier in its lifetime, it would have been harder to kill. We could have brought out a version with fewer features earlier. From that point on in my career, any software development schedules I developed used a phased approach with lots of demonstrable milestones along the way. They included time for test software for the early phases of implementation before many of the parts could be integrated.

I also learned from this disaster that I was not very good at dealing with, or even recognizing office politics. The hardware architect of the system's (over-complicated) hardware felt he knew how to design software and manage it. I had a strong suspicion that he was not rooting for me to succeed. I came to the conclusion while working at Amnet that I was pretty good at managing downward although I needed improvement, but I was clearly not good at managing sideways nor upwards. I wanted to go back to being an implementer, or at most a 'hands-on' project manager. I wasn't ready to throw in the towel yet at Amnet, but Eric threw it in for me. I was demoted and the hardware architect took over the management of the X.25 project.

It was time for me to lick my wounds and move on. Before leaving the company I spent some time looking into and designing a method of keeping the network's distributed and replicated database concurrent.

Chapter 13

Go West Young Programmer

After returning from Costa Rica, I realized that I was not a cold-weather person, even though I grew up in the Boston area. I had always dreamt about living in California. Now seemed to be a good time for that.

I flew out to Silicon Valley and had a number of interviews. I landed a job with Olivetti in Cupertino. This was their Personal Computer division. It was at the beginning of the Personal Computer industry and before there were any standards. It was just before IBM announced its Personal Computer (August 1981) and after Bill Gates' historic agreement with IBM to keep the rights to the PC-DOS (MS-DOS) operating system that he implemented for IBM. He actually bought an existing PC operating system, QDOS, from Seattle Computer Products and modified it for IBM. Microsoft bought the rights to the software from Seattle Computer Products for $50,000 without telling them of the pending deal with IBM. Gates proceeded to make his first fortune as a result of this licensing agreement.

Olivetti is an Italian company, known mostly for its typewriters. The president and many of the higher ups in the company were Italians. I was hired by and reported to Gianluca Rattazzi. I wouldn't be surprised if the spelling of my last name helped me get the job. Gianluca wasn't a transferee from Olivetti, Italy, as many were, but rather an Italian who was hired while living in the states. It was mostly a good situation. Great weather. I got a house only 10 minutes away from the office so did not have the horrible commute that many had in that part of California. Gianluca was a great boss. He liked to delegate.

The only downside of working at Olivetti was that I was hired as manager of the PC software communications and networking group. I really didn't want to be a manager again, but doing so got me to California. There were a number of projects going on in the group: asynchronous communications, synchronous IBM 2780/3780 and 3270, SNA and LAN. It kept me busy for a couple of years. During that time my wife gave birth to our third child, a girl. Actually, she was pregnant when we moved to California - an amazing woman to agree to a move like that with two two-year olds in tow and another on the way.

There were certainly some differences between working in Silicon Valley and the Route 128 Boston corridor. Both were areas with lots of startups fueled by universities such as Stanford in Palo Alto and MIT in Cambridge (blocks from my father's dry cleaning store). But the startup fever was a lot higher in Silicon Valley. One of the software engineers working in my group at Olivetti would usually keep his office door closed (we all had real offices with doors – nice). One day I walked in on him and it was obvious he was working on something other than Olivetti work. I had suspected for some time that he was not a full loaf. One day he fixed an urgent customer-reported problem in an asynchronous communications package. The president of our subsidiary asked me if I thought we should give the engineer a bonus for his work in solving that problem. I told him I didn't think so. I didn't tell him why. Soon after, that engineer left Olivetti to start his own company.

Another day while sitting in my office at Olivetti, I heard what sounded like a freight train drive within a few feet of the office. It was an earthquake, California style. It was LOUD and therefore scary. It was different than the earthquakes I'd experienced in Costa Rica. They were much more friendly. The building swayed gently, the windows rattled, the computers shook, but there was no loud noise. Actually, when I was a kid lying in bed one night in our house in the Boston suburbs, awake because it was so hot, I swear I felt the earth move. Sure enough, it was reported in the next day's paper that a small earthquake had taken place. I read once that earthquakes can come in cycles and those cycles can be hundreds of years apart. The Pilgrims in Plymouth, Massachusetts experienced a major earthquake on the 2nd of June in 1638. I wonder.

Although it was a lot more crowded in Silicon Valley, I found the driving easier in many ways than in the Boston area. California is simply a lot newer and the roads are better planned. Many more wide two-lane secondary roads. I experienced lots more road rage in the Boston area than in Silicon Valley. Maybe because of the poor design of the roads there, many folks have trouble figuring out who has the right-of-way in any given intersection. Or maybe they believe they just always have the right away.

Most of the time I'm very laid back and easy-going, but an inconsiderate driver can bring out an aggressiveness in me that surprises me. I believe that I do know the right-of-way laws and don't enjoy it when someone violates my right-of-way! On one of my recent visits to the Boston area, I remember several incidents. I was on Route 2 in Acton. I don't remember the exact situation, but I did not yield my valid right-of-way to a young couple that was trying to take it from me. In stereo, in exact unison, they both flipped me off. Another time I was driving up the hill on Toten Pond Road in Waltham. It's not a minor road. A woman starts backing out into the road in an SUV with kids in the back seat. I guess she expected me to stop for her but I didn't. I slowed down to pass and when she saw that I wasn't going to yield the right-of-way to her, she stopped. As I drove by her, she was looking into her rear-view mirror and clearly, succinctly, mouthing the word "asshole".

As I get older I get mellower and such incidents occur less frequently but I still have some work to do in that area. Luckily, driving in Las Cruces, New Mexico, where I now reside, is reasonably sane. And that's what I felt about driving in Silicon Valley - it was sane. But then I had a short commute and didn't have to drive on the freeway to work. I was just driving in California a few weeks ago (Walnut Creek, Davis) and it felt the same to me – crowded but sane. I didn't lose it once. When learning to drive in Massachusetts, we were certainly taught well the legal right-of-way laws. However, we would jokingly say that in practice, the driver with the oldest car has the right-of-way.

After a couple of years, major changes were taking place at Olivetti in Cupertino. IBM PC software was becoming standard so software tasks became porting software written for the IBM PC to the Olivetti PC. Gianluca and other good people within the company were leaving. I wasn't ready to leave. Before Gianluca left, I convinced him to transfer me into the Advanced Technology Group. Out of management, finally!

Somewhere along the line I became interested in the PICK operating system, built by Dick Pick. I think it was because of its similarity to the system I worked on in Costa Rica. It was a highly efficient and reliable demand-paged, multi-user, virtual memory, time-shared operating system with a built in dictionary/hash-file based database, high level language (PICK-BASIC) for implementing (mostly) business applications, a PROC procedure language for executing scripts plus a database query language (ENGLISH). Would have been perfect for implementing our Costa Rican applications.

One of the reasons I found the PICK system so interesting was because of its popularity and portability. It started out on minis and had been ported to mainframes and most recently to micros. It was being used all over the world and is still in use today. Among other projects, I convinced

Olivetti to let me explore the possibilities of building a bridge between a PC and a PICK system. I started working on a prototype but the working environment was deteriorating every day.

The final straw was when I was told I would not get a promised bonus. I was told the reason was because I was no longer a manager, but I think it had more to do with the fact that the head of personnel hated me. The personnel department at Olivetti had an unusual amount of power when it came to things such as hiring, firing, promotions, raises and such. Maybe that was an Italian thing, although the head of personnel was an American. I had a number of run-ins with her. One in particular was when she was opening my incoming mail. I explained to her that I didn't want her opening my mail and that, in fact, it was a federal offense to open someone else's mail without permission.

It was during my stay at Olivetti that the Apple Macintosh was announced. Being a manufacturer of PCs, Olivetti got a hold of a few when they first came out. I got to take one home for a while for evaluation. One couldn't help but love the technologically advanced user interface. My twin sons were three years old by now. They sat down with the Mac and were proficient with it in days. One of the boys didn't know at that time that it would lead to a career as a software engineer, following in the footsteps of both of his parents.

One of the highlights of working at Olivetti is that I got to meet and lunch with a couple of extremely bright and interesting guys who were working there at the time in the Advanced Technology Group. The first was Piero Scaruffi. He was doing some heavy-duty research in area of Artificial Intelligence. According to Wikipedia, Piero is a historian, philosopher, poet and scientist. And there was Gerard Bucas, a South African who had transferred from Olivetti in Italy. He was a pioneer in the development of digital public packet switching networks and distributed network operating systems. He went on to become the VP of Engineering of Commodore Computer (the Amiga computer) and is now CEO of Scala Broadcast Multimedia, which is a leader in the field of Digital Signature Software (google it).

During my career, I watched a number of colleagues move up the ladder to the top spot of a company. That was not in the cards for me. When I tried it at Amnet, I found I did not have the strengths (or political stomach) for it. And I realized that I really enjoyed building products. But there are many in the industry who don't realize when they have gone beyond their potential (the Peter Principle). I've seen a lot of company founders who are good at starting a company but are not capable of bringing that company beyond a certain size. Either they lack the skills or simply aren't interested in learning the necessary skills. Many realize their limitations and bring someone into the company with the right experience. Others are forced by the stockholders to do it. But of course there are some that can start a company from scratch and stay with it through every step of the way to becoming a large corporation. That's one of the things that I admire about Bill Gates.

Chapter 14

Back to Beantown

After two and a half years with Olivetti in Cupertino, it was time to move on. For some dumb reason, I started thinking about moving back to the Boston area. I think it had to do with it being a better place for the kids to grow up. It was close to relatives and the schools were really good back east. It was closer to Germany, but I think the German relatives preferred visiting us in California than in Massachusetts. The software job market was still good (it had never been bad since I started my career) and it didn't take long to find a company that would relocate us back to Massachusetts.

Technical Communications Corporation (TCC) was a small company that built and sold data encryption devices for use on synchronous and asynchronous communications links, and in some cases were protocol sensitive (HDLC, X.25, TCP/IP). It was a public company but the president and friends owned controlling interest. His three sons worked in the company. I was hired as Software Manager, but it was a small group of five software engineers including myself. It was definitely a 'hands-on' position. I would oversee the design and scheduling of all the products/projects in our group, but would always have my own product to implement.

During my four years as Software Manager at TCC, we built a number of encryption products, each one always more powerful and feature rich than the last. There were usually two parts to each project: the device itself, and a

Crypto Management System running on a PC. In addition to the requisite communications ports, each device would have a front panel with a small keypad and display for configuring and servicing the device (i.e. running diagnostics). There was also a 9-pin port for communicating with a terminal (or PC emulating a terminal) in a command line mode. This was simply an alternative way of configuring and servicing the device. Configuration parameters could also be entered at the Crypto Management System along with encryption keys. The parameters and keys could then be loaded into a SmartModule and loaded into any number of encryption devices via the 9-pin port. Later versions of the Crypto Management System, which I will talk about later, would manage encryption devices in real time over communications links.

I learned a lot about software development while at TCC. My software development skills and productivity improved dramatically during those years. Two of the reasons were the 'C' language and the PC. It's obvious that writing in a high-level language is going to take less time than writing in assembler (generally thought to be five times faster). The other great advantage of 'C' is its portability. It allowed us to implement a lot of software for the encryption devices on a PC, which for a number of reasons goes lots faster than implementing on the target hardware (i.e. prototype hardware availability, hardware bugs). It did require us to implement some device simulation software on the PC for those functions close to the hardware such as the front panel I/O, but the time spent was well worth it.

Using PCs, we could also simulate the communications link between two encryptors with RS232 communications drivers in the PC. I could implement and test all hardware independent software, including communications protocols, without the target hardware. In some cases the engineer implementing the communications hardware dependent software would use a PC to test out his software by developing test programs on a PC that would exercise all the functionality of his hardware dependent software. Several times we integrated our two pieces of software, hardware independent and hardware dependent, without a hitch as our respective pieces had been well tested before integration.

PC simulation can greatly speed up the debug and test process. And having your own dedicated PC for compiles and assembles can really speed up the development process, especially for those of us who, unlike the debug-averse engineer I worked with at Nixdorf-Entrex, don't write code that works the first time around, (or the second, or the third ...).

With such quick 'compile and go' turnaround time, it was also cost effective to do 'unit' testing on the PC. For example, it was easy enough to write some code that accepted input from the keyboard and could be used to test individual modules or functions, throwing at them both valid and invalid inputs and making sure the functions behaved properly and that the outputs were valid.

It was during my years at TCC that I felt that my software design skills improved considerably as well. I found that top-down design really worked for me. At times though, I would get tired of the design process and feel that I wanted to see some tangible results, so I would jump ahead and do some bottom-up implementation.

I implemented a lot of products from scratch at TCC so had plenty of design/implementation experiences. The design phase was always top-down, but the implementation (coding) phase would be mixed. Maybe I'd want to implement a lower level function to make sure some assumptions I had made about it were correct. Or maybe I'd implement it because it was a fun function to implement and I needed a break from the hard stuff. Often though, I'd implement from the top putting in stubs for the yet-to-be implemented lower level functions. But when I didn't, I could easily test out lower level functions with some throwaway test software so I didn't need the upper level software to unit test the lower level software.

All of the code that we produced at TCC for its encryption devices was embedded code. After compiling or assembling the code on the PC, we would copy it to the PROM (Programmable Read Only Memory) of a computer chip such as a Motorola 68000. The PC sends the executable file to a PROM programming device, which in turn writes or 'burns' the code into the actual chip. So the process is now: compile, write to PROM, and go (debug/test). But having both a dedicated workstation (the PC) and a dedicated PROM programmer, turnaround time was still quick, and contributed greatly to our productivity.

Having your code in read-only-memory of course implies that code and data (constants) in ROM cannot be modified. You would think that no programmer in his right mind would want to modify code, but I'm reminded of a programmer at Entrex, the one who designed the awkward-to-use range check feature, who wrote code that modified itself. His cute little 'programming trick' of modifying an assembly language instruction, presumably to save a few memory locations, certainly made it difficult for me to find and fix a bug when troubleshooting a problem at a customer site in the U.K.

At TCC I got to work closely with hardware engineers in defining new products. We were constantly coming out with newer and better encryption devices. Which features should be done in hardware versus software? In general, anything extremely time-critical, like encryption, would be done in hardware. Some of the standard low-level communications protocols were already implemented within the communications chips. But sometimes you don't want the hardware to be too smart. It's simply a lot easier and cheaper to change software than it is to change hardware. So you don't want to go overboard in the hardware design.

In an ideal world, a software development group would have a library of functions or routines that could be used to build new products. That may work for some applications but it didn't work for us. Sure, some general-purpose functions such as a command line interpreter could be used in different encryption devices, but each new product would have new hardware and software features and it didn't really work. However, we would still implement the software in a very modular and structured way. We had coding and documentation standards.

One thing you can count on about a piece of code that you write is that someday it is going to be changed. Well-structured and documented code is simply easier to understand and change. And it may be you someday that comes back to a piece of your own code written several years earlier and benefits from the amount of documentation you put in.

We practiced many of the coding techniques that are inherent in C++, which hadn't yet appeared on the scene. For example, each module had a well defined set of inputs and outputs, and all other modules could use only those inputs and outputs and not access anything within the module (encapsulation). In that way, the module could be changed, except for the already defined inputs and outputs, and would not affect other modules that use that module. New inputs and outputs could be added, but existing ones could not be modified.

So when building a new system, it was easy enough for us to take modules from existing products and add the newly required functionality to them. Cut, paste and modify. Implementation of new products went quickly. Also at times it would be necessary to add functionality we put into newer products, back into older products. This would work because of our implementation methods. Well-structured and documented code - thank you Chris W.

A few comments about comments. Firstly, comments should be useful and describe the *why* and not the *what*. I saw a comment once "add A to B register". That was pretty obvious from looking at the instruction itself. It's hard to believe someone would enter such a useless comment, but it happens. Maybe the programmer was being paid so much per comment line. Also I would recommend keeping documentation as close to the actual code as possible. If it's in a separate document, it's less likely to get updated when the code is changed. When writing code in C++, I would put most of the documentation in the .C module and not the .H module because that is the first place a programmer is going to look when troubleshooting a problem in a piece of code or simply trying to understand the code.

In the earlier days of computing, programs were hand written and often typed onto keypunch cards by operators. It didn't matter that many programmers could not type or were very slow typists. That changed as we started to enter our own programs via terminals. That could be one reason why many programmers didn't include a lot of documentation with their code. When in my junior year in high school, for a number of reasons (one being I was flunking out of Italian class), I made the decision to change from the college course to the business course. In my senior year I took a typing class. It was a good thing in more ways than one. I was the only guy in a class full of female juniors. I learned to touch type during that year and improved my typing skills further while in the Air Force. Part of my job was to transcribe the Polish Air Force chatter captured during the day onto 6-ply paper during the midnight-to-eight shift. Sometimes on those mid shifts when there was not much to do, we would have touch-typing speed contests.

Who could type "Now is the time for all ..." ten times with few or no errors in the shortest period of time.

Once programmers started to enter their own programs on terminals such as teletypes, typing lots of documentation didn't affect my productivity but I could understand the reluctance of other, two-finger typists, to add lots of comments to their code. It's a different world today. My son, the software engineer, can type as fast as I can never having had any formal keyboard training. I'm not sure how many fingers he uses, but it's certainly more than two.

There were some not-so-memorable moments at TCC. At one point, my counterpart, the hardware manager, quit. Software department was doing really well. We were meeting our deadlines and the customers were happy with what we were producing. So Arnold, the president, asked me to manage both the hardware and software engineering groups. I would report directly to Arnold. Firstly, I was very comfortable with my hands-on position and had no desire to move up into management. Once was enough. Secondly, I understood hardware enough to do my job. I could implement any device driver, but I couldn't read a schematic. I'm a liberal arts guy. Thirdly, not many people had the right skills to report directly to Arnold. Many who did found themselves out the door after a not-so-long period of time. I told him I would do it temporarily until he found someone else. He wanted me to make a permanent move.

It didn't take long for Arnold to realize that I really wasn't the right person for the job. So I happily went back to my old position. If I had agreed to take the position permanently, my move may have been out the door instead of back into the software group.

They eventually hired a VP of Engineering. What I remember about him is that on my first performance review, he gave me really low marks on my 'people management' skills. That of course wasn't true. Everyone in our small group was happy and productive. I felt that at that time he considered me competition for his position, which was the reason for the poor review. If he only knew. My people management skills improved on my next review once he realized I had no interest in moving up the management ladder. Politics.

There were also some memorable moments from my days at TCC. One of the products I worked on was sold to the CIA. I got to go to their headquarters in Virginia and demo and test the encryption device with their equipment. I spent several days there. It reminded me of my days at NSA. A bunch of great people working there. For the most part, the people I met and worked with at both agencies were just nice people, good people dedicated to their jobs, families and friends. A lot of what we see in the movies about the agencies is a lot of hooey. For example, as far as I know, NSA (we never said "*The* NSA") does not do Human Intelligence (HUMINT) but only SIGINT (Signals Intelligence), which includes other -INTS including COMINT (Communications Intelligence – what I did in the Air force), ELINT (Electronic Intelligence – i.e. telemetry signals), RADINT (Radar Intelligence) and LASINT (Laser Intelligence). HUMINT is the domain of the CIA.

I also got to work on a product sold to a group at NSA. I got to make a trip to the agency for a meeting with that group. It was exciting. I enjoy revisiting people and places of the past. I set up a luncheon with former co-workers who were still working there. It was good to see them again and I was having trouble tearing myself away from the luncheon. I did so at the last minute. I gathered up a co-worker who had accompanied me on the trip, the VP of Engineering (the guy that gave me bad management marks on my performance review), and we left the restaurant headed for the agency. I missed the correct exit from the Baltimore-Washington Parkway for the agency and we were late. The VP of Engineering and others were not happy about our lateness. However, I was enjoying myself so much that day that I didn't really care.

While working at TCC, another 'management' weakness of my mine became clearly evident. At TCC and previous companies I made a number of hiring decisions. One day while at TCC I reflected on all those that I had hired and realized that I had only about a 50% success rate. Only about half of the people I hired turned out to be good, productive engineers. Reliably picking good people was just not a skill I possessed.

My greatest achievement at TCC, and the second greatest achievement of my career, was a project for the Egyptian military. One day I was told that Arnold's son Jim, one of the salesman, made the largest sale in the company's history. It was a network of T1 encryptors and a network management system for the on-line management of those encryptors. Jim promised the customer all kinds of features and capabilities that the company had never implemented before, along with delivery dates, all without ever consulting with the software department. To his credit though, he told me simply to tell him what we could do and in what time frame we could do it and that it was his job to sell that to the customer.

I came up with a full year project, the first six months implementing the encryptors, the last six months spent on the network management system software. The encryptors could work without the network management system. Encryption keys could be generated by a program on a PC, written to a SmartModule, and then loaded into any number of encryptors. Encryption keys could be synchronized between encryptor pairs via encryption key initialization protocols. Servicing the encryptor could be done via the front panel keypad and display. Unlike an asynchronous encryptor I worked on earlier where encryption was done entirely in software, encryption was done in hardware.

In both the earlier system I worked on and this one, the core operating system was a round-robin, event driven executive responsible for such tasks as scheduling and executing automatic Encryption Key changes, servicing diagnostic and key management requests from another data encryptor or from a Key Management Station, scheduling and running background diagnostics, logging and reporting errors and alarms, and servicing the encryptor's front panel keypad and display. Thank you once again Entrex. Interrupts were only used on the communications ports (don't want to lose characters).

The Network Management system was comprised of redundant PCs communicating with the encryptors over dedicated asynchronous links. From a key management station one could remotely manage the encryptors performing such tasks as downloading keys into the encryptors, scheduling Encryption Key changes, and running diagnostics. There were several Network Management Stations, each with two PCs, one being a hot standby ready to take over if the primary PC failed.

I felt that to complete this project on time, we would have to put in some long hours. I walked into Arnold's office one day and told him about the aggressive schedule and suggested that he should consider giving us bonuses as an incentive to meet our deadlines. He thought about it for a few days and decided to give everyone in the company a bonus if schedules were met.

Well, to everyone's surprise, we met our deadlines. Most surprised were the sales people who said they had never seen a software project of this magnitude finish on time. Additionally, the customer was extremely happy with the results. This was a multi-year sale (adding additional hardware in later years) and brought the revenues of TCC from $3 million a year up to around $15 million a year. I felt my participation in the project contributed greatly to its success and hence my feeling that this was one of the most significant accomplishments of my career.

How did we manage to come up with a realistic schedule and then meet it? Starting point was simply asking ourselves the question "What level of functionality can we deliver within the specified time frame?". This may sound like the obvious thing to do, but more than once I've seen people design the 'ideal' system and then try to squeeze its implementation into an unrealistic time frame.

Some of the other reasons the schedules were met include: 1) the quality of the engineers working on the project; 2) the software development methods we used as earlier described (the ability to reuse and easily enhance existing, well structured and documented code); and 3) our heavy use of PCs for debug and test purposes. The hardware simulation and test software that we wrote for our PC's allowed us to test our own pieces without having to wait on hardware or another persons software to be working. It made critical path scheduling a lot simpler.

We put in a few weekend days during the final implementation phases, but we were never seriously behind schedule. All of our product goals were met, however, our implementation schedule was such that the least important features (highest levels of functionality) were at the end of the schedule. If we were late and had to deliver the product on a definite date, we could have simply left out some of the least important features. Or worst case, on the missed delivery date we could have demonstrated a working system with n levels of functionality. Our implementation schedule included a series of milestones, each with a higher level of functionality.

Head of software at TCC was a good fit for me. Yes, I was a manager, but it was a small group (usually four or five). I always had my own hands-on project. I was doing well managing downwards, having learned from my mistakes at Amnet. Being a small company, there was very little politics to deal with, which I still was not good at.

I had responsibility for and enjoyed all phases of software development from starting with a blank piece of paper to ending up with a finished project. I especially enjoyed the beginning, the initial design of the product (in some companies more of a marketing function), and the end, when delivering the product to a satisfied customer.

To me, the implementation phase of a product was just a process, although an enjoyable one. Some engineers seem to be more interested in the process itself rather than the product. Throughout my career I ran into a number of software engineers that seemed to be more interested in learning and using sophisticated programming methods rather than building a product. To me, a programming language, like 'C', was just one more tool in getting the job done. I'd learn just enough of a programming language to get the job done. I'll talk more about this later when I start using C++ as my primary language.

Chapter 15

First Business Venture

Shortly after starting to work at TCC, I began moonlighting nights and weekends on a project of my own. After having spent two and a half years in Silicon Valley, I guess some of the entrepreneurial fever rubbed off. I took the knowledge I gained during my last months at Olivetti and built a Pick/PC bridge product (P~Bridge). My wife, an accomplished software engineer who had not yet gone back to work, would help.

The product we built allowed a PC running MS-DOS (Windows didn't exist yet) to be locally or remotely connected to any computer running the PICK operating system. It supported PICK terminal emulation, file transfers between the two operating environments, and the ability to create and modify PICK items (records) on the PC.

My goal was to just implement the product and sell it to one or more of the many value-added distributors of the PICK system. I advertised in PICK trade journals. There was lots of interest in the product from all over the world, mainly because there was no other product like it in the market at that time. But I couldn't find a company to buy the product - possibly because of my lack of marketing/sales skills.

One day I lunched with one of my co-workers from my Entrex days who had become CEO of several companies and I let him convince me to sell directly to the end user. Mistake. I sold a few systems but didn't really have the time or the stomach for dealing with end users.

I enjoyed designing and building products, but really wasn't interested in, or capable of, selling them.

Chapter 16

Let's Try this Again

When I returned from California four years earlier, it was November and Massachusetts was very gray and starting to get cold. It didn't take long for me to ask myself why the hell I moved back. I had forgotten how much I disliked the climate, not just the cold winters, but the many days without sun. So, I don't know how I did it, but I talked my wife into moving to California again. She would not move back to the South Bay area because of her fear of earthquakes. So after pouring over earthquake maps, we came up with Davis, California. A university town. A 'green' town. Could I find work there? Not really, but I convinced TCC to let me consult for them, long distance.

We bought a 20-foot motor home and slowly made our way cross country having an adventure along the way. This time we kept our house and rented it out. We rented a house in Davis. I paid for the moving of the household goods with my TCC bonus. I had a couple of PCs, bought a PROM Programmer, and was in business.

During our year in Davis, I Implemented a FIPS-140 compliant version of the X9.17 Encryption Key Distribution Protocol. During implementation, I could debug and test the protocol by dialing into a test port of NIST (National Institute of Standards and Technology). I also implemented the firmware for an M68000-based modem-implant board providing encryption services for a Radio Packet Switching Modem. Both fun projects.

Davis is a great place to live and bring up kids. It is a very environmentally-aware city. Being more inland than Silicon Valley, winters are colder and summers warmer. We didn't have nor need A/C while living in the San Jose area. Summer evenings were cool there. In Davis, there are more houses with swimming pools that can be used during those hot summer evenings. A/C is a must. We were living in Davis during the 1989 earthquake that caused the double-decker Cypress Freeway to collapse. We felt the quake 70 miles away.

Chapter 17

Time to Settle Down

I tried to convince TCC to allow me to set up their 'west coast' development center, but they wouldn't have it. I couldn't work for them out there for much longer and there were really no jobs for which I qualified in the Davis area. So it was back to our house in Massachusetts. We're going to stay put this time until the kids finish school. I decided it was time to become a contract software engineer. I incorporated for tax purposes.

My first contract was with, who else, TCC. They were beginning to implement a network of IP (Internet Protocol) encryptors for a U.S. government agency. The project also included a Network Management System, similar to the one I had implemented for the Egyptian military. This time though, they felt they needed to implement it on a Unix workstation. I questioned the need for the extra expense and complexity involved in its implementation. One justification I heard was that it was a requirement by the customer. It may have been, but I got the feeling that they didn't try to sell a PC-based system. They could have taken the existing system and cut-and-pasted a lot of code and built a new one.

I had the feeling that part of the motivation for implementing a Unix-based system was that some people wanted to see 'Unix' on their resumes. TCC was still a small company with no Unix expertise. It was no surprise when the system was delivered long after the promised deadline. They hired some not-so-competent Unix programmers and in addition to overkill in the hardware selection, there was also overkill in the software design. Were they designing software functions that they wanted to see on their resume, or were they simply not good at software design and were over-designing? In either case, the company suffered.

Later on in my career I came to believe that there are lots software engineers who over-design. They cannot think 'simply' (KISS). One software engineer I worked with was a very detail-oriented programmer. He was great when working close to the hardware where there were not many decisions to make. No one was better at writing device drivers. It may have taken him a little longer to implement a device driver, but when done it was rock solid and complete. He didn't miss a detail. When he was asked to implement software at higher communications layers, his code became overcomplicated and convoluted. His being extremely detail-oriented became a disadvantage at the higher layers. He over-designed his code. He couldn't think simply when it was necessary to do so.

One of the things that occurred to me at TCC was that we all have our strengths and weaknesses and that it's best when a manager recognizes a person's strengths and assigns that person to tasks that match those strengths. The above mentioned detail-oriented engineer had problems working with another manager who felt that as a senior software engineer, he should be able to perform X, Y and Z, which was part of his job description. He was asked to design and implement some higher-level software and it simply didn't go well. I'd hire that individual again in a minute, assuming I could utilize his strengths in the task or tasks at hand.

It was also not uncommon to find software engineers who would under-design. This was especially true when it came to writing code at the user interface level. More than once I found I could easily crash a system by inputting something that wasn't expected. An example of this is when a programmer doesn't put in a buffer overflow check and simply holding down a repeating keyboard key would crash the system. Sometimes the programmer's response when confronted with this type of problem would be "Well, the user is not supposed be doing that!". A lot more 'defensive' programming is required at the user-interface level. For me at least, the closer to the hardware (the further from the user), the easier the software design task. There are just a lot more unknowns to deal with at the higher levels.

How does an engineer know what the right level of design is for a particular product or project? Some will want to implement the minimum of functionality, possibly because they are being judged on how quickly they finish or because they aren't enjoying this task and want to move on to the next. And there are those who want to add all kinds of bells and whistles to a product, maybe because it makes the project more interesting for them.

Many engineers don't like to have to worry about budget or time constraints, but those variables have to play an important role in the design process. What or how much can I do within the specified time frame and with the specified resources? After having been through this a number of times, I would try to design a product so that there is an appropriate level of functionality to meet the deadline and product requirements, but also design it so that additional possible future enhancements may easily be added – design A, B and C, but only implement A and B for now.

I'm now reminded of another point of view in favor of an initial minimalist approach in implementing a software product. When implementing my first real product, the NSA Intelligence Collection system, the manager of our group offered a sage piece of advice. He said that in the initial release of the product, I shouldn't worry about implementing all of the bells and whistles that the end user thought he wanted. He said to give them a working system that met all the major requirements, let them use it for a while, and then let them tell us what they *really* want the system to do.

Obviously there are many variables to take into consideration when designing and implementing a system to include things like the expected life of the product and the sophistication of the user. A piece of prototype-only software or software that would only be used once (i.e. test software) need not be as well designed and implemented as a piece of software with a long life expectancy. And the less computer savvy an end user is, the more bulletproof and easy-to-use the user-system interface needs to be.

Back to my Unix project. Aside from having to deal with some not-so-competent Unix software engineers on this project, I enjoyed implementing Async Connection Services allowing the Unix-based Network Management System to dial up and carry on diagnostic/key distribution sessions with a network of T1 data encryptors. For both the Unix and embedded platforms this included: an Open/Close/Send/Receive API (Applications programming Interface) for the management of connections; modem dial/answer services; a reliable data link protocol, and low-level I/O interfaces (Unix TERMIO, Motorola 68302 communications chip device driver).

Chapter 18

Second and Last Business Venture

While doing contract work for TCC, I got the bug to again build and sell a product of my own.

Entrepreneurship was in my blood. My father had flat feet and was rejected by the army when he tried to enlist during World War II. So he started his own dry-cleaning business. He was an experienced presser at the time. He started by going door-to-door in his neighborhood asking the occupants if they wanted their clothes cleaned. He lived on Sunset Road in Cambridge and he named his business Sunset Cleaners. He started out on a bicycle. Over the years he built it into a successful business. He had a free-pick-up-and-delivery route that encompassed a number of cities in the Boston area. He opened a store in Cambridge and later another in Belmont. The second store didn't last too long because he didn't have the business skills to manage two stores. He was a hard worker and output a quality product. Those were his strengths.

His father, my grandfather, also had his own business. In Italy he was a wine barrel maker. After he came to this country he was a toolmaker. In his later years he would push around a homemade cart with several large sharpening stones. He would go from neighborhood to neighborhood with his cart and sharpen people's knives and scissors. He'd leave his cart at his last customer's house at the end of the day and take the bus or streetcar home and come back the next day. So it was time for me to try again. It was in my blood.

I built an asynchronous communications product for a PC. It allowed the PC to establish dial-up connections with other computers and carry on an interactive chatting session or transfer files using the common protocols of the day, Xmodem and Ymodem. I called it "EasyComm". It had a graphical user interface using the PC's graphics characters that allowed the creation of boxes or windows. It had extensive help tools including a built-in user's manual (no paper documentation required). It had a small footprint (98K) and was extremely easy to use. Options, such as setting the communications parameters, were all done from menus. It allowed the generation of macros for such things as dialing telephone numbers. It was written in 'C' with the communications device driver and interrupt handler written in assembler. It was a neat little product.

This was 1991 and pre-windows. My marketing strategy was to sell it to modem manufacturers or resellers who would bundle it with their modems. They would pay me a couple of bucks per sale. I sent off a bunch of letters with demo versions of the product and didn't hear from a single company. Needless to say, after that I never had the urge to build another product of my own. I did make use of EasyComm though in later projects.

I had been working for TCC in different capacities for about eight years now. It was time to move on. One reason is because the current software manager and I weren't on the best of terms. We didn't see eye to eye on some implementation issues and I'm sure my successes at the company made his failures look worse than they were.

Chapter 19

A Matter of Software Management

I got my next job working through a contract software agency. It was with Digital Equipment Corporation (DEC) in Stow, MA. They had built an asynchronous statistical multiplexor that was used at a network management station to communicate and carry on diagnostic sessions with remote DEC computers (I don't remember the application of the remote computers - I think it was classified). I was tasked with basically improving the performance and reliability of this device. I was brought in to head up a project tasked with bringing out the next release of this product.

It's kind of unusual for a contract engineer to come into a company and manage regular employees. Normally a contractor is brought in as an individual contributor. The software manager turned out to be a woman who joined Amnet a few weeks before I left for California. I'm surprised that my record at Amnet didn't scare her off.

I first spent some time learning the system and getting to know the skills of the four software engineers on the project. It was clear looking at the software and talking with the people that what was lacking in the earlier implementation of the product was good software development management. Two of the software engineers in the group were part of the original implementation team, one of who implemented the core operating system. Both were relatively inexperienced junior programmers. A third engineer was from inside the company but was recently added to the team. The fourth was another contractor recently brought in to help with the project.

Next I built a tool for evaluating the performance or throughput of the multiplexor. I took EasyComm, the asynchronous communications program that I had previously written for the PC, and modified it to allow me to pump bytes into the multiplexor on one port and receive them on another port, varying transmission speeds. How many bytes could I pump through without losing bytes on the receiving ports and at what speeds? Bytes lost were easily detected as I was sending a fixed pattern over and over. I could also set up multiple PCs in order to test the simultaneous transmission of data over multiple ports.

After evaluating the people and the system I decided that we could increase throughput by making a number of smaller modifications to the existing system rather than re-writing large portions of the system, which is what we software engineers would usually prefer to do. It's definitely more fun to rewrite.

There were a lot of problems with the core operating system. It processed the transmission and reception of data under interrupt control, but the interrupt control routines were inefficiently written, or over-written. They were easily optimized which helped gain increases in throughput. It was an event-driven O/S like the Entrex system, but contained lots of unnecessary code and was easy to shrink and optimize. And that was without affecting the reliability or robustness of the software. A major problem with the O/S was that it was PASSing (context switching) too often.

Another problem was that the protocol control bytes used to encapsulate data packets as they were transmitted was much too verbose. We eliminated unnecessary packet overhead, which helped greatly in increasing throughput.

There were a number of other small changes we made (which I don't remember anymore). We'd make a change and then test it with the modified version of EasyComm to see how much the throughput was improved. In the end, we improved throughput by a factor of 20. Yes, that's 20 times faster. Throughput (with no characters lost) went from about 1900 bits per second to about 38000 bits per second.

One of the main challenges working on this project was managing the team. I didn't write any code for this project except for modifying EasyComm. I spent a lot of time analyzing the system, coming up with the necessary changes and schedules, and assigning the appropriate tasks to the appropriate engineers.

The one junior engineer who had worked on the O/S was assigned to modify/optimize some of the code he had written. He wasn't thrilled because it meant changing some of his design. (He was too junior to be designing such important time-critical software in the first place, which I felt was, again, a software management problem). He had to be told exactly what to do and was not too happy or too productive.

The senior contract engineer in the group turned out to be useless. He was one of those engineers who was more interested in the software development process rather than the product itself. I couldn't think of anything for him to do. I didn't feel he had the right skills to help achieve our goal of improving system throughput. I felt he was more likely to do the opposite.

The other junior programmer was assigned to making the system more user-friendly. The user/system interface was improved. Better diagnostic and error reporting.

The fourth programmer, John Temte, who actually moved over from a hardware engineering position, was a total gem. Not only did he implement many of the changes that I identified, he came up with many on his own which contributed greatly to the throughput improvements that we made. He worked in all parts of the system including the O/S. Maybe in another situation, such as designing a new system from scratch, he wouldn't have shined. But in this case, he was indispensable! I couldn't have done it without him. The point being, again, that we each have our strengths and a challenge for any manager is to recognize those strengths and put them to good use. I was getting better at that.

DEC was very happy with the results of the project. They asked me to get up in front of a group of managers and talk about the project. Not something I really wanted to do. Not something I was used to doing. Somehow I found the courage to muddle through and was surprised when I was told it went over really well (probably the only time a talk I gave went over well). I was told how they were all impressed at how the decision was made not to re-write but rather to make lots of small changes. The project lasted five months.

Chapter 20

First Call in Downtown Boston

Finding my next contract position took a while. It was the longest period I went in my entire career without working - three months. As a contractor, I felt I had to be choosy in selecting my projects. I had to make sure I would do something that would help me get my next contract. Something that would broaden my experience. Something that could make me more valuable. The main reason I became a contract engineer was so that I could make good money while working as an individual contributor. No more management!

After three dry months without work I accepted a position that was not ideal. I almost backed out of it at the last minute as I was offered another, better contract days before I started working on the accepted contract. I told the woman at the agency that the newly offered project was a much better fit and I wanted out of the contract. She went ballistic and intimidated me into fulfilling my agreement.

The position was with Thompson Financial, located in downtown Boston. The job was to design and implement asynchronous connection services allowing PCs to dial up and access Thompson's First Call broker-sourced equity research information system. It was similar to the async software I implemented for TCC's network management system. It turned out to be a fun year. In addition to implementing the async connection services between PC's running DOS and the information system's Unix server, I got to implement the async software for the Macintosh and

Windows O/S. Like at TCC, I implemented an Open/Close/Send/Receive interface for the applications programs on all platforms to communicate with each other. In some cases it also included low-level I/O device drivers.

This project didn't do a hell of a lot for my resume, but it was fun. I thought commuting into Boston would be a hassle, but it wasn't. Firstly, I worked at home most of the time, and secondly I would usually drive partway and take the subway the rest of the way. It was nice taking lunch breaks in Boston during summertime. The manager I reported to was great, an Irishman from Ireland with an Irish brogue living in an Irish section of Boston. He knew how to delegate. He once described my code as 'elegant', a trait I clearly inherited from Chris W. Another happy customer.

Chapter 21

What's an Internet?

My next-door neighbor was responsible for helping me get my next contract. He was a high-level software manager at Sun Microsystems. One of his groups was working on Internet related PC communications software. The head of that group was one of the team members in the Nomad group that I managed at Nixdorf-Entrex as well as a team member in the X.25 group that I managed at Amnet. Small world.

I was hired to implement the PC-based client side of the Kerberos authentication protocol. A database of user authentication information (password, access permissions) resided on a network server (most likely Unix at that time). The user entered his user id and password on the PC, and then the protocol was used by the PC to communicate with the server for the purpose of authenticating the user. Kerberos was popular with educational and governmental institutions. The RADIUS (Remote Authentication Dial-In User Service) protocol, which was similar to Kerberos, was the authentication protocol of choice for the business community.

This was my first introduction to Internet communications software. I also ported a number of Internet utilities written in 'C' to the PC (PING, RSH, RCP, RLOGIN). At this time the Internet was in its infancy in terms of public access.

Just where did the Internet come from? Back in 1970, the Department of Defense created a 4-node network, the ARPANET, connecting three universities and one private company. It was primarily meant for resource sharing. In 1975 the first commercial packet-switching network, Telenet, which was a civilian equivalent of the ARPANET, came to be. At Nixdorf-Entrex, we used the Telenet X.25 network to test out our Nomad geographically-distributed database product. In 1983 Arpanet split into Arpanet and Milnet, the latter being a military-only network. The World Wide Web came about in 1990 when the HTML language was created which in turn allowed the creation of browsers providing access to websites on the Internet. The ARPANET was renamed the "Internet" in 1995.

The contract with Sun Microsystems lasted five months and the experience gained helped me to get my next contract.

Chapter 22

Devil's Advocate

I was hired to implement the client side of the RADIUS authentication protocol for one of DEC's remote network access products. This was at a branch of DEC in Littleton, MA. So far during my six years as a contract engineer, I had had only successes. This contract would change that.

There were three of us involved in the project. First was the project leader, who had already completed a design of how RADIUS would fit into the system. I was the one with the responsibility of the actual software implementation. The server side of the software already existed. And then there was a senior engineer whose job it was, I think, to consult on the implementation of different products. As best I could figure, his job was to find fault or holes in someone else's design or implementation of a product. That's all I ever saw him do. He seemed to keep the design of the system in constant flux, always coming up with new problems, never solving any of the existing ones. I suppose it's good to have someone play devil's advocate at design reviews, but as far as I was concerned, he was keeping the project from going anywhere.

The project leader, who was his senior, quit. That left the two of us. I eventually got frustrated with making no progress and started implementing according to the departed project leader's design. At that point in my career, I was also no lightweight when it came to designing a software feature and how it would fit into a system. I went ahead and got a demonstrable, prototype version of the RADIUS client up and running. The consulting software engineer was now playing more of a role in the system since the project leader had left. He was still re-designing the system. I had had enough.

I found another job through a contract agency. I gave my notice at DEC. They weren't happy. They brought in another contractor to take over my part. A high level manager asked me to hold a meeting to go over the design of what I had done so far. I went into the meeting unprepared. I was a short timer and lacked motivation. I just wanted to leave. She had expected to see some formal design documents and I didn't have any. I described the system on the whiteboard. She was upset. The consulting engineer was grinning. I came off looking like an ass.

I actually did have an informal design document, more of an 'object oriented' diagram of all the pieces and how they fit together. It was a more detailed iteration of the project leader's original design diagram. The contract engineer who took over the implementation asked me why I didn't bring it to the meeting. I hadn't thought to do so. Hopefully she showed that document to the manager and the work that I had done to that point had not been for naught. The consulting engineer took over the project at that point so I expect that my software wasn't used. Can't win them all.

Chapter 23

A Startup with a Stock Option

It was now 1995 and the Internet was starting to heat up. I saw my future in Internet communications software. I knew it was going against my strong preference of staying 'small', but that's where the money was plus I enjoyed working on communications and networking protocols.

I was offered a contract at Cascade Communications Corporation, a fast growing company in Westford, MA. They manufactured WAN (Wide Area Networks) communications switches that pumped data through the Internet. I jumped at the opportunity and quickly forgot about my experience at DEC. I was brought in to, what else, implement the client side of the RADIUS protocol for their WAN switch.

Briefly, a Cascade switch could support up to 16 processors, each on its own card, including up to 14 I/O communications processors and two control processors (one being a hot-standby) for handling control functions such as the RADIUS client. I/O processors could handle an array of communications software/hardware, protocols and speeds (T1, E1, Frame Relay, ATM, SMDS, ISDN, TCP/IP, HDLC, async) intermixing those variables in one 'multi-service' switch. Data could arrive in a switch encapsulated in one protocol and leave the switch encapsulated in another (i.e. Frame Relay to ATM).

A Sun Microsystems Unix workstation was used to manage the switches via the SNMP protocol. In addition to the switching of data through the network over virtual circuits, switches also had strong routing capabilities. The author of the OSPF (Open Shortest Past First) Internet standard routing protocol, John Moy, was an employee of Cascade. John has written several books on OSPF and MOSPF (Multicast OSPF). OSPF became the first widely used routing protocol on the Internet.

Cisco Systems was a competitor of Cascade. Cascade was the leader in 'switching' data through the Internet and Cisco was the leader in 'routing' data through the Internet although Cascade's switches could also route, and Cisco's routers could also switch. (Strictly speaking, 'switching' is a communications layer 2 function, assuring delivery of data between two points along a communications path, whereas 'routing' is a communications layer 3/4 function, assuring delivery between two endpoints of a communications path such as two IP addresses or users sitting at their PCs.)

The RADIUS server, which I was to implement, would reside on the Central Processor (CP) in a switch. Like the hardware for the Amnet X.25 switches, these switches contained multiple processors that had to communicate with each other. Unlike the Amnet hardware, the Cascade switch hardware wasn't over-designed or overkill for the task at hand. But it was still a multiprocessor system and bringing up a new software load, debugging and testing it on that platform could be difficult to say the least. Not because of flaky hardware but more because of the software development methods employed (I will talk about that later).

I didn't want to have to deal with debugging my code while at the same time learning a new system and dealing with the problems associated with bringing up a new software load, so I first implemented the RADIUS client on a PC. I also wrote the software in C++, which was new to me. By implementing first on the PC I simply eliminated having to deal with so many variables at once. I tested it together with the RADIUS server running on one of our Unix workstations. I then ported it to the switch's CP at which time I spent the time to learn the process of bringing up a new software load and working with the switch's software development tools.

This would be a good time to talk about my thoughts on C and C++. I loved moving from assembler language to C. I became so much more productive. I could debug and test code on a PC or a Unix workstation before porting to the target hardware saving lots of time and aggravation. But as I've said before, a computer language is simply a tool used in the process of building a product. I wasn't crazy about the fact that in C one could perform the same function in different ways such as when dealing with arrays and pointers. One way would have been enough for me. As I've said, I learn just enough of a computer language to get the job done. I would look at another engineer's code and not easily understand it because he or she chose a different subset of the language to use.

C code can be very cryptic. An argument for providing all this flexibility in C is that one coding method may produce more efficient code than another. For one, that would depend on the compiler. There are two issues with efficiency: time and space. Nowadays memory is cheap enough so that it should not be an issue. If there are timing constraints, then the most efficient way to handle it is to write the time-critical function in assembler. Another option would be to take the assembler language output from the compiler and optimize it. That approach worked well for me in implementing an async communications device driver for a PC as well as a heavy-duty encryption algorithm running completely in software in an encryption device sitting on a communications link.

All this flexibility was not a major problem with C, but C++ is a different story. I've never heard anyone other than myself complain about this problem in C, but many have the same objection with C++. I know what the designers of the language were trying to do. They were creating a tool that allowed programmers to write more structured, object-oriented code. That's a very well intentioned goal, and I'm a big fan of object-oriented design and coding, but one can write well-structured, object-oriented code in C. With C++, one can write totally unintelligible code using such features as virtual functions with abstract classes. Maybe it's just me. The more abstract something gets, the more difficult it is to understand. Now, those engineers who get off on 'the process' rather than the product, love this kind of stuff.

As previously mentioned, if there's anything definite about a piece of code, it's that it will someday need to be modified. Software is never static. So a major goal in writing software should be to make sure it is easily modified. What does that mean? First of all that it is easily understood. Second is that it should be well-structured so that it can be modified without affecting other pieces (objects) in the system. When enhancing or modifying a piece of poorly written code, sometimes it is more appropriate to throw it out and rewrite it than to try and modify it. Rewriting could be faster and hopefully the end result would be easier to modify in the future.

At both Nixdorf-Entrex and TCC we wrote coding standards with one of the benefits of those standards being that one engineer could pick up another engineer's code and easily understand it. It all boils down to 'productivity'. That being said, I enjoyed writing code in C++ and a major advantage of the language is that it forces engineers to write more 'object-oriented' and 'structured' code, but I wish the designers had kept it a lot simpler (KISS).

After completing the RADIUS project, I was given another assignment at Cascade. I was to take some existing PPP (Point-to-Point Protocol) code and make it work over an ISDN (Integrated Services Digital Network) link. Briefly, ISDN allowed digital transmission of data over regular copper wire telephone lines but at higher speeds than with asynchronous modems. It was eventually superseded by DSL. As part of the project I implemented a number of PPP related protocols from scratch (PAP/CHAP, BAP, IPCP and MLPPP). I became Cascade's resident PPP expert. I thoroughly enjoyed working on this protocol and felt it was a really good fit for my interests and skills.

At that point I was asked to become a direct employee of Cascade. Why did I accept the position after almost seven years of being a contract software engineer? For one, Cascade, as well as other companies at that time, had dual promotion ladders, one for management and one for individual contributors. I could stay an individual contributor with the same salary increase opportunities as a manager. I was also offered a good size stock option. And I was enjoying the work.

Chapter 24

Cascade Becomes Ascend

Not long after I joined Cascade, they were bought by and became Ascend Communications (1997). Ascend was a west coast company selling high-density dial-up communications equipment (ISDN, DSL, async) to such companies as AOL and Earthlink. That meant they no longer needed our ISDN communications capability along with my PPP software, although PPP was eventually used in the switch with other communications hardware (Frame Relay, ATM), so it didn't go away.

I worked on a lot of different projects at Cascade-Ascend during the next five years. Some tasks included: enhancements to the TCP/IP BSD stack; implementation of a debug trace facility for IP, SNMP and PPP packets; implementation of SNMP agents/MIBs and console CLI configuration for a number of protocols; and implementation of a logging server.

A major project I worked on was a Policy Based Forwarding feature. This feature allowed IP packets to be selectively forwarded over cut-through Policy (QoS – Quality of Service) PVCs (Permanent Virtual Circuits). There were three parts to this feature: 1) the creation and maintenance of the distributed/replicated policy database, 2) the establishment of the QoS PVCs which supported ingress/egress port types of IP over ATM, Frame Relay, PPP and Ethernet, and 3) the selective forwarding of data over those PVCs. Policies were based on the contents of the IP header information (i.e. source or destination IP address, type of protocol, type of service). It started off as simply being a small feature for one customer but then it grew into a more comprehensive, general-purpose feature that could be compared to Cisco's Policy Based Routing feature.

I spent a long time working on this project. Testing it was a nightmare. This would probably be a good time to talk about the many different software development problems at Cascade-Ascend. First I should say that I feel most of the problems were caused by the lack of good software management. I blame the managers at all levels. There were a lot of talented engineers in the software group. They were just victims of poor, or a lack of, software management.

For example, there seemed to be no concept of 'ownership' of a feature or piece of code. Anyone could change any code at anytime. I had never seen anything like this before during my entire career. If I'm the implementer of a piece of code I feel responsible for that code. If there are problems with it, I want to fix them. I'm the best person to fix them as I know the code better than anybody. If someone finds a problem in my code (which they seldom did), or want an enhancement made, they should come to me. If I can't do it at that second and they need it right away, they can do it under my guidance.

I'm also particular about my code (thanks to Chris W.), so I prefer that someone else not degrade it either aesthetically or structurally. Some pieces of code are almost a work of art. I take pride in the fact that my code is well thought out, well documented, well structured, well tested, easy to understand, robust and reliable. In the early days of Entrex, before Nixdorf, the software manager at that time made the comment that if he wanted something to be implemented "quick and dirty", which at times is necessary, then he would give that task to programmer X. But if he wanted it done for the long haul, he would give it to me. He recognized our strengths and used them appropriately.

At one point during a minor reorganization in the software group, I found myself working for John Moy in the routing group. John is one of the most brilliant engineers I have ever met. I came out of a talk he gave on routing protocols simply in awe of his knowledge and understanding of the routing world. A lot of what he said was just too complicated for my simple mind to comprehend.

While in John's group, I was tasked with implementing a protocol (IGMP) that provided services to routing protocols such as John's OSPF protocol. I implemented the protocol and after unit testing handed it off to another engineer in John's group whose software would determine that IGMP ran flawlessly the first time with no bugs (that didn't always happen). As good object-oriented coding practices dictate, I provided one set of functions (API) through which access to all IGMP functions would be made. By not allowing someone to directly call functions within the IGMP code, I could change those non-callable functions without worrying about affecting anyone else's code. (Although I wrote IGMP in C++, I had to provide a C interface because some of the software calling it was written in C).

Knowing how there were no restrictions on anyone changing anyone else's code in the software department, I asked John to come to me if he wanted any changes made in the IGMP code. I would be happy to change the API to accommodate his requests. Well, not long after that I found myself in a different software group. Asked why, I was told that John would rather have someone working in his group that doesn't already have an established style of coding.

John, who in addition to being the author of OSPF, was also its implementer. Having seen some of his code, I'd just say that his coding abilities nowhere near matched his design abilities. The company would have benefited from having John spend more of his time designing than implementing. That goes back to the point that we all have our strengths, and weaknesses. I could never design, let alone completely comprehend, a routing protocol that allowed an email to find its destination halfway across the world in a matter of seconds.

There was another result of the no-ownership policy. One of the reasons I joined Cascade as an employee is because I thought I would be the person responsible for PPP and all future enhancements. Well, another PPP related project came along, and I was free to work on it, but it was given to another engineer in our group. That engineer wanted to gain PPP experience and he simply had a better relationship with the boss. I liked my boss, but I never went out of my way to make points with him other than by doing good work and meeting my deadlines (which hopefully made him look good). I always felt I could get by on my ability to get the job done, and get it done well. And I'm sure it didn't help that I was not always the most tactful or loyal employee. (In fact, some would consider me inflexible!)

I suppose I was somewhat inflexible, set in my ways after thirty years developing software and having mostly successes along the way. My boss wasn't happy when I complained about having to fix other peoples broken code when that person was available to fix it himself. It had to do with ownership as well as having to deal with extremely poorly documented and written code. Just looking at some of the code in the system made my blood boil. Again, I felt it was a software management issue. The goal was always to implement a feature as quickly as possible. Engineers were rewarded for meeting aggressive deadlines.

Writing well-designed, documented, structured and tested code was not a priority and not rewarded in this company. As a result, there was lots of really bad, poorly documented and un-maintainable software in the system.

An engineer would make a change to a piece a code and break two other pieces in the process. Eventually they got to the point where more time was spent on, and people involved in, fixing problems than on adding new features to the system. Okay - using this approach gets new software features done more quickly in the beginning, but later on so much time is spent fixing problems that adding new features take much longer to implement. And it doesn't take long to get to the point where the earlier gains in time are lost and you'd be ahead of the game if it were done properly in the first place. "Quick and Dirty" doesn't work for the long haul.

Another result of the no-ownership policy was that in some cases there were no clear lines of separation between major software functions, or objects, in the system. For example let's take the System Initialization process, which was no small task. No one owned this important piece of the system. Anyone who needed something initialized simply made a change to this process. As a result, after doing a new software build in order to test some new software, quite often the system would crash during the initialization phase. You had to debug it before you could ever get to your own software. If someone owned that code, and used better programming practices in maintaining it, it would be easier to maintain and would be more reliable saving other software engineers time and aggravation in bringing up new software builds for testing.

If the system had been broken down into more well defined and structured pieces (i.e. terminal user interface services, SNMP services, PVC services, O/S services, database services) and each piece were owned by one or more engineers, and each piece had a life of its own with its own unit testing before being put into a new software build, then software builds would be a lot more stable providing a much more productive development environment.

And a final result of the 'no ownership' policy. Because no one group or person was responsible for providing a consistent user interface, the end user suffered. I'm talking primarily of how users would set and modify system parameters. There were two main ways to do this: either at the network management station via the SNMP protocol, or via the CLI (Command Line Interface) from a connected workstation. Whenever I implemented a feature, such as IGMP, RADIUS or Policy Based Forwarding, I was responsible for defining the SNMP MIB entries and for defining the corresponding CLI commands. Every engineer would define (and implement) his own. There is no way that the syntax of commands or MIB parameters would be consistent among the different features implemented by different engineers.

There were virtually no rules of how to add commands. It was a free for all. There was consistency throughout the features I implemented, and in some cases I modified the CLI for other features making them more consistent with mine, but that was still only a fraction of all the system features. Consistency is a very important factor in providing a really good user interface. If, for example, a CLI is consistent in it's command syntax, it becomes intuitive for a user to enter commands for which he or she may have forgotten the exact syntax. We used Cisco routers all the time for testing our switches. Cisco provided a consistent CLI.

Back to the nightmare of testing my Policy Based Forwarding code. Testing the code in the CP was easy. It was the code for maintaining the Policy database. The tough part was in the I/O cards that contained the actual forwarding of the code over a Policy PVC, performing any protocol conversions along the way. This was a 'multi-service' switch supporting all types of ingress and egress port types (i.e. PPP, ATM, Frame Relay, Ethernet). The problem was that most of the forwarding code was junk. It was poorly written and documented. Some called it 'spaghetti' code. There was one software engineer who wrote excellent 'forwarding' code, but only one that I can remember.

Working on 'forwarding' code was for me something to avoid at all costs. Just looking at it made me sick. Unfortunately, because of the lack of ownership and the practice of all engineers encouraged to work on whatever code necessary to get his task done, I got to spend a lot of time in that code while testing all the different ingress/egress port types and protocol combinations. Eventually all combinations were working. That was until someone made a change to the forwarding code that broke my code. After a major software release was distributed to customers, a basic fault was found in the Policy Based Forwarding feature. It turned out someone had made a change at the last minute to some forwarding code that was used by my code. It took me several days to find and fix the bug. Another fun day at Cascade-Ascend which at about this time became Lucent Technologies (1999). If they only knew what they were getting themselves into.

Chapter 25

Ascend Becomes Lucent

For my last year and a half or so at Lucent I worked in the Routing group. John Moy had left the company and one of his protégés had taken over. I was intimidated by the complexities of the routing protocols, but was anxious to learn what I could. Maybe it was all those Friday night beers and my 29 years of smoking cigarettes (quit 14 years earlier) that killed off some of my brain's learning cells, but I was simply having difficulty wrapping my mind around those protocols. Perhaps my meager math background had finally caught up with me and was affecting my ability to grasp those complex routing algorithms. Maybe it was my age. In a couple of years I'd be sixty. Also, I seemed to have a mental block when it came to learning new things. I was slowing down.

One of my sons started working at Lucent as a software engineer in his sophomore year of high school. He worked there for three summers. He first sat in front of a computer at age three and both his mother and father were software engineers, so he had an early start. He was an Internet and Linux internals expert and some of the projects he worked on included an IP security audit on the Lucent switch fixing many of the uncovered weaknesses, an IGMP packet generation tool, an IP packet flow generator, virtualized a BGP implementation to run on a Linux platform, assisted in porting OSPF and ISIS switch simulators to Linux, and provided the company with on-call Linux support. Some really heavy-duty stuff.

Unfortunately, I told my son once about Chris W's 30-hour day (20 awake, 10 asleep), so to the consternation to his co-workers and family, he spent one summer on that schedule. The pace at which he completed his projects made me feel old and that I was really slowing down.

At this point in my career, I'm getting tired - tired of the short-term thinking and management-by-crisis mentality of many of the American companies that I've worked for in the recent past. But I'm not quite ready to call it a day.

During my last years at Lucent there was lots happening in my personal life. I split with my wife of 22 years. People change and being a good deal younger than me, she changed lots more. Must have been the exposure to all that new age stuff during the times we spent in California! It was an amicable split. And then I was diagnosed with prostate cancer. Not being one to make rash decisions (the urologist who ordered the biopsy wanted to cut out the prostrate right away), I needed time to evaluate all the treatment options, and there were plenty. It took a while to organize and set up tests and meetings with the specialists and to evaluate the different options (surgery, radiation, brachytherapy, cryosurgery, hormone therapy, chemotherapy, combinations of some of the above). Luckily I was living in the Boston area with some of the best doctors and hospitals in the world.

During the time between being diagnosed with cancer and deciding on a treatment, I was worrying about the cancer spreading while being untreated and started getting extremely anxious. My doctor prescribed Valium to help me get through that period. While I was taking Valium I was assigned to a project to build a prototype of a streaming video application. It meant modifying the IGMP protocol, which I had originally implemented. The application involved allowing a user to turn on or off the reception of a video (feature film) over the Internet.

I eventually chose a treatment plan that is pretty much the same plan that Andy Grove, former CEO of Intel, chose. It worked for him and it worked for me. I am still cancer free. After I came off of Valium, I took a good look at the code I had written for the streaming video prototype and couldn't believe how awful it was. It was the worst code I have ever written in my life. Extremely bad design. Valium did a job on my ability to think clearly. But I fixed the code and moved on. By the way, during my treatment Lucent couldn't have been more understanding and helpful. There were no complaints about all the afternoons I missed for radiation treatments.

While in the Routing group, I was tasked with taking over an implementation of the up and coming standard protocol for multicast (transmitting from one to many) routing, PIM (Protocol Independent Multicast). OSPF was a unicast (one to one) routing protocol. A version of PIM was originally written at Lucent's office in Great Britain. I kept busy enhancing and debugging that version of the protocol as well as supporting software I had previously written such as RADIUS and Policy Based Forwarding.

It was just about this time that the company started having its financial problems. They started well before other Internet software and hardware companies began having their problems, which eventually led to the collapse of a lot of those companies. Engineers started leaving the company. The manager of the Routing group left. I was asked if I wanted to take over the group and I answered with a resounding "no". A relatively junior engineer took over the group. I helped out by taking on the responsibility of all multicast routing software support which meant continuing work on PIM as well as troubleshooting problems in other multicast protocols (MOSPF, DVMRP).

At one point Lucent stock price was over $60 a share. With my stock option and shares bought through the stock purchase plan, I was worth over a million dollars (before taxes) on paper. Unlike other employees who would periodically sell some of their option shares as they vested, I was greedy and assumed the value of the stock would keep going up. When the Internet bubble burst, Lucent shares fell to about $2 a share. I watched them gradually drop over a period of time not believing that their value could just keep on dropping day after day. I never sold during that period. Luckily, earlier I had sold enough to add to my kids college fund so that I could put them all through college.

My salary at this point was obscene. Up until recently there was a real shortage of software engineers in this country. That's why we, like other high tech companies, brought in a lot of employees on H1B visas. In the Routing group of about seven people, except for me, all were from India, Taiwan or the People's Republic of China. After Lucent bought us out, they stopped giving us regular cash merit bonuses but instead, so as not to lose people, they gave us large salary increases.

After my Lucent stock became almost worthless, there seemed to be no reason for me to stick around any longer. Work had not been enjoyable for quite some time. Many of my associates had already left and gone to other companies. Eventually when things got really bad, Lucent had it first layoff. I found out that I was not on the list of folks to be let go. There was plenty to do in the Routing group and I was still the Policy Based Forwarding and RADIUS guy. But when I heard the terms of the layoff, three months salary and six months health insurance, I convinced them to put me on the list. Some lucky person was taken off the list. At this time, my kids were either starting or already in college. It was time for me to head back to the land of sunshine and warm weather. I decided to move to San Diego.

Months earlier, just before Lucent started having its troubles, I was in California and I stopped in the Lucent (formerly Ascend) office in Alameda. One of the software engineers from our group had transferred there about six months earlier. I visited him at work and chatted with some software managers. They would be happy to have an extra body in their group. Alameda would be a great place to live. But just as I got back to Westford the company stopped all hiring and all transfers. I was out of luck. Bad timing.

Chapter 26

Go West Old Programmer

A few months later, several months before I left Lucent, just as things started to go south within the entire industry, I organized some interviews with several companies in the San Diego area. I didn't get any offers. I think there were several reasons. One is that the positions being offered were going away while I was there because of the current industry problems. Second is that they would always ask about my current salary which was a non-starter for these companies. I would try to explain to them that the salary was not important and that I would accept less, but I don't think that helped.

Finally, I don't think I interviewed very well. In two places I was asked to write some code on the whiteboard given a specific problem. I was told I did all right by one interviewer, but at another company I didn't do very well at all. I was asked to write some C++ code for a doubly-linked list. Truth is, in my later years, I didn't write lots of original code. First of all, I carried around with me a library of useful functions that I had written over the years. When needed, I would reuse a function or if it didn't fit the exact need of the new function, I would cut, paste and modify. Or I would use a standard library function that existed within the system on which I was working. Seems to me that a company would want to hire an engineer that didn't always have to write new code to accomplish a software task.

Also, I was never good at coding, designing, or even problem solving on the fly. I was not good at meetings where this took place. I would take a problem or feature request back to my office, sit down, put my feet up on the desk, and play with it for a while until I came up with a solution that I liked. And usually it was a better solution than any that were proposed on the fly. Again, it's the 'quick and dirty' versus the 'better long term solution'. I'm just not capable of the quick and dirty solution. Maybe it's because I'm a Libra.

So for sure I lost at least one of the interviews due to my inability to think on my feet. And I'm sure that inability worsened as I got older. So, I take Lucent's layoff package and head out west. Part of that package was a pension cash-out, which wasn't much, but I didn't even know I had a pension. I have no complaints at all about how I was treated at Lucent.

Just a few more observations about Lucent before I head out west. First, like other companies developing software, Lucent started outsourcing some of its software to India. They tasked software engineers in India with the maintenance of releases of the products that were out in the field. The idea was that they would do the 'dirty work' of software maintenance or 'sustaining' software development while we focused on the development of new features and software. In doing so they were carrying their no-ownership policy, along with all the aforementioned related problems, to the extreme. Just what are they teaching in the Computer Science graduate and undergraduate programs nowadays?

When I think back to my days at NSA and Entrex, and how those of us that worked together also played together, I realized how much the social environment had changed over the years, especially during the last five or so years. Most people at Lucent were not interested in getting to know their co-workers socially. They came to work, did their jobs, and went home. The few times I went out for a

Go West Old Programmer - 116

few beers after work it was more often than not with a co-worker from my Entrex days. I suppose part of it was a cultural thing. More than half of the software engineers were imported from other countries.

Unlike the old days when we would chat about all kinds of topics, talk at Lucent focused more on the state of the company and the current price of its stock. Maybe it's that a company like ours, a startup, attracted a lot of engineers motivated mostly by money - high salaries, large stock options, and large bonuses for meeting deadlines. Maybe that's why there was so much focus on pumping out code as fast as possible with little regard for the quality or longevity of that code. Again, I guess it is part of our culture.

When I think of quality versus quantity, a couple of parallels come to mind. One is the fact that Japanese cars are *still* consistently of higher quality than American cars (although I'm reading good things about the Ford Fusion!). One of my co-workers at Entrex told me that he had a software contract with General Motors (early seventies). The task of the project was to help design a vehicle's air conditioning unit that would last for three years but not necessarily longer than three years. It only had to last long enough for the warranty period.

Another example is the difference between an American and a German house. While in Germany I saw a number of homes that were being built or that were just built. The quality of an American home just doesn't compare. The German roof is tile and lasts forever. Windows are of the highest quality and will never need to be replaced. Walls are cement with colored stucco (verputz) on the outside requiring very little maintenance. Sure, houses cost more in Germany. Many Germans would save for half of their lives to be able to afford to build a house, and then live in that house for the rest of their lives.

So I sold my house, put my household goods in storage, and drove out to San Diego, visiting several Air Force buddies along the way. I eventually found a house to rent near the beach in Encinitas, just north of San Diego. There were not many jobs that matched my Internet experience in the area, but there were a lot of companies that dealt with embedded software (firmware) or communications software, two areas within which I had tons of experience. I could get back to 'small'! I spent three months there but never found work.

The software industry was melting down. More bad timing. At least I missed the cold Boston winter. My unemployment checks were about to stop coming in. I drove back to the Boston area and moved in with relatives. I contacted several companies where former Lucent employees were now working. No luck. Former managers that I worked for couldn't, or wouldn't hire me, and I know there were open positions for which I qualified.

I never did find a job during the next year. In addition to there being very few jobs around, I think there were possibly a number of other reasons I couldn't find work - my age (which my former co-workers now knew), last salary, being considered a possible health risk (cancer could return), and the impression I may have left with co-workers that I could be 'inflexible' (due to my strong views on software development methodology that I didn't always keep to myself!). I would have liked to work a few more years before retiring, but that was not to be.

Chapter 27

A House on a Lake

Fortunately, I saved enough money so that I didn't really have to work again. In a couple of years I could start collecting Social Security benefits. I took the money from the equity in my house and bought a house on a lake in Florida. One day I simply went on the Internet, eBay real estate to be exact, and looked for a lakefront house in a warm climate that I could afford. I found one in Florida and got on a plane and checked it out. I didn't end up buying it but bought another in the next town on the next lake.

At about this same time two of the software engineers that were in the Nomad group at Nixdorf-Entrex were also in the same situation. One is about five years younger than me so had a ways to go to Social Security, but he had been a successful contractor for many years, had no children, and saved a good deal of money. He simply retired and is now enjoying his new life with his wife in their new home in Tennessee.

Another engineer was not so lucky. He put two kids through college, one who is now a doctor. He couldn't retire. After a while he got a license to drive big rigs (CDL) and did that for a number of years until recently when he finally got a software contract position.

I am still in contact with the members of the Nomad team and we occasionally get together. It is harder nowadays since we are so geographically dispersed. Two members of the team married each other. You can bet that when those of us who found ourselves without jobs get together, one of the topics of conversation is the outsourcing of jobs to India. Or the fact that many jobs in our market segment were being held by lower-paid H1B visa engineers. Is uncontrolled globalization really the best thing for America?

I'm currently reading Tom Friedman's book "The World is Flat" which makes a convincing case for globalization, and he's right in saying that we can't stop it, but perhaps we need to manage it better. Outsourcing jobs to India is one thing, but bringing in more H1B visa engineers to fill jobs that could be filled by higher paid qualified Americans is another.

Over the years I've worked closely with engineers from many different countries. One major difference I've noticed between American engineers and all others is that, in general, American engineers tend to be more creative and innovative than their foreign counterparts. As a result, they tend to have better system design abilities. Building a product is both a science and an art. Chris W. is a perfect example of that. His simple idea of creating a general-purpose language for data entry batch balancing applications greatly enhanced the flexibility of the Key-Edit product. His implementation of that language was a work of art.

Another example of this is the difference between Entrex's simple yet powerful operating system and the German Nixdorf's failed attempt at creating a data entry operating system to replace the Entrex system. They simply copied the design of an existing IBM operating system. The Entrex operating system was truly a work of art. There are probably a number of reasons why Americans are the way they are. In Tom Friedman's book, he believes that "one reason that America has always been a leader in the innovation of products and services ... is that our society has always valued (*both*) technology and liberal arts".

Chapter 28

Reflections of an Old Programmer

There were a lot of changes in the computer industry during the 35 years I was a software engineer. The two most significant were the introduction of the personal computer (and the standardization of its hardware and software) and of course the Internet. I'm amazed at the rapid technological advances made in the industry during those years.

During the seventies, only companies, and not individuals, could afford to buy small computers, and those computers would only have up to 64 thousand bytes of memory. Today I can buy a personal computer with four billion bytes of memory. Our disks at Entrex could only hold up to 11 million bytes of data. A PC's disk today can hold over 500 billion bytes.

I never got tired of designing and implementing software. I truly enjoyed it. I never got anywhere near burnout. I think that's primarily because early on I realized my strengths and my limits and never allowed myself to be put in a position where I couldn't excel - well almost never. Another reason is because there was always something new and different about each project. There was always something new to learn. It has been a fun ride.

Over the years I worked for both large and small companies. Both have their advantages and disadvantages. In a smaller company you are more likely to make a more significant contribution. You may end up wearing a lot of different hats allowing you to learn more. There are simply fewer people doing more tasks in a small company. There's typically (but not always!) less politics in a small company.

I just think back of some of the differences in working for the young Entrex as opposed to working for the older, only by about four years, Nixdorf-Entrex. At Nixdorf-Entrex, I worked on the Nomad project for about two years before it was cancelled. It bothered me that I spent two years for naught. That would never happen in a smaller, one product company. In larger companies, they may have two separate groups competing by building the same product. The better or more politically connected one would win. The other would go by the wayside.

I felt NSA was a good place to start my career. More opportunities to learn and not as much pressure to deliver. It also provided a great social environment, allowing me to make many good friends. It would have been a great place to spend the last years of my career if the weather in Maryland weren't so bad. I actually sent NSA my resume during my last attempts to find work before deciding to retire. I said I would be interested in working for them again, not in Maryland, but somewhere with a warm climate. I never heard back from them.

I've worked on all sizes of products, from hand-held devices to mainframes to the multi-processor Lucent switches. As I've already mentioned, I've always preferred small, mainly because of the amount of control I had over the product. Being the only or lead engineer working on a product, I could assure a consistent user interface. Also, the smaller a product or project, the simpler and quicker it is to implement.

Some of the companies I worked for along the way did not understand, and found out the hard way, that on larger projects, adding more engineers can increase the implementation time exponentially. For example, doubling a project from two engineers to four does not mean cutting the implementation time in half. The more people working on a project, the longer the design and implementation phases take. There will be more time spent in meetings because of the additional opinions and ideas that need to be considered. A higher level of communications, including more detailed documentation, is required because of the additional paths of communications. Debugging and testing take longer, for one because usually there is only a fixed amount of equipment available for that purpose. As the old saying goes, you can't make a baby in one month with nine guys.

Any large and complex problem can be broken down into a number of smaller, manageable pieces. Object-oriented design techniques are excellent tools for accomplishing that goal. Lucent's software would have benefited greatly if better software development methods had been used.

This story wouldn't be complete without some words on resume writing. After working in the industry for a number of years I was faced with several resume-writing challenges. For one, I was determined to keep my resume to two pages, which I've always been told is desirable. Next, I didn't want it to look like I changed jobs a lot, which I did at times early in my career. I solved that problem by simply not including the oldest jobs on my resume. Experience I gained years ago wasn't relevant to the current job market so I wasn't losing anything. My knowledge of the ALGOL programming language wasn't going to help me find a job in the Internet era.

Another reason for dropping those earlier jobs off of my resume was that it hid my real age. Fortunately I could pass for someone ten years younger. People at my last job, Lucent, were surprised when I told them my age (not sure why I did). I was certainly the oldest software engineer in the company. I was always honest about my experience on my resume, but took some liberties with dates. I didn't have a degree but I did include "BA in Modern Languages, 3 years completed" at the very end of my resume. Not having a degree never really hindered my career. The experience trumped the lack of a degree. There were many others of my generation without degrees and some had degrees but not in Computer Science. A copy of my final resume is in Appendix I.

And what can I say about job hunting? I guess I was an advocate of the 'shotgun' approach, especially when it came to working with headhunters. I would simultaneously work with multiple agencies, whereas other engineers I knew would work with just one or two. The agencies I would work with didn't seem to mind, or they didn't tell me if they did. I kept strict track of which agencies had brought which job openings to my attention. The first agency that had mentioned a specific job opening with a specific company was the only one that I would deal with for that position. I used that same strategy as a contract software engineer.

Early in my career, a lot of the jobs that I got were through people I had worked with in the industry (i.e. the Entrex crowd). But that didn't work in my later years, probably because both I and the industry had changed. As one gets older, one becomes more 'extreme' in one's views. As mentioned, I had less tolerance for poor software management practices in my later years (i.e. allowing lots of crappy, poorly documented code to be implemented in order to meet a deadline) and was more likely to voice my opinion. Also, I was never super-loyal to any of the people I worked for. And it just got worse as the years went by. My loyalty came from respect - respect for that individual as a manager, and I just didn't come in contact with many good managers in my later years.

I'm reminded of the day I had my re-enlistment talk with an Air Force officer. He was a respected, former fighter jet pilot. I had no issues with him. I really enjoyed the work I was doing and if I had re-enlisted, I could have gone on to learn more languages and lived in more interesting places. I told the captain that the main reason I could not re-enlist was because I'd have to work for people like ... and I gave him the name of a sergeant who I was currently working under. He was simply incompetent at his job. His main contribution was to bring in sandwiches for the troops during the midnight-to-eight shift. That would have been a positive thing except that he sold them to us for a considerable profit. That's not to say we didn't have very competent sergeants-in-charge, but, like the government, people move up in rank whether they are competent or not.

I look back at all the different companies I worked for. There certainly were a lot of them, especially early in my career. Many job changes had to do with wanting to live somewhere else. Some people move to another state or country for a better job opportunity. I moved because I wanted to live in that other state or country.

There was one job offer I had that I wonder if I made the right decision by not accepting. When it was time to leave Olivetti in Cupertino, I interviewed with a company in Monterey, California. It was a company selling some sort of weather system built on Data General Novas and involved lots of communications and networking software. I had all the right experience and was offered the job but turned it down. My wife and I loved that part of California. We would spend vacations there.

The main reason I didn't take the job in Monterey was simply because there were almost no other software jobs in the area which fit my skills. Odds were that I wouldn't stay with any one company for a long time. It was much safer to work in either the South Bay area or the Boston Route 128 corridor. That's where the majority of jobs were for the type of software that I enjoyed and for which I was qualified.

I've included a copy of a C source module in Appendix II that I wrote for the EasyComm product that I built and never sold. It's an example of the type of documentation I've included in my code throughout the years. It's really old code and my coding style changed and hopefully improved since it was written. In those days I redefined some of C's conditional and logical operators primarily for readability purposes (Grace Hopper would have approved).

After living in Florida for two years I decided to try out the southwest. I exchanged hot and humid for hot and dry. I moved to the Land of Enchantment, New Mexico. I found my Shangrila in Las Cruces. Good size city, friendly people, good climate (virtually no snow), and great Mexican food. Life is good ...

I just returned from my neighbor's house where we had a few beers and some grilled burgers. While sitting at the table eating my burger, his cat was circling my right leg. I felt something bite me. I stood up and what appeared to be a small bug fell out of my pant leg when I shook it. I then felt another bite on my knee. I shook harder and a 3-inch centipede fell out. The cat's prey.

My neighbor, a Las Cruces policemen and member of the SWAT team, stomped on the centipede with all his might. If you're reading this, then you know I've survived. Research on the Internet says I'll most likely live but will have to endure some pain – a bad bee sting (a really LARGE bee!). I've found several scorpions in my house, but they were either dead or close to it thanks to Ortho Home Defense Max, which I faithfully spray around the perimeter of the house. Again, I'm told their sting is no worse than a bad bee sting. One day I helped my elderly neighbor on the other side of my house kill a small rattlesnake she found in her yard. I guess that comes with living in the desert. Time to apply ice again...

Appendix I – Final Resume

Overview

Extensive experience creating, modifying and porting (mostly real-time embedded) software with emphasis in the areas of communications, networking, I/O drivers, O/S internals, and security. Comfortable in the role of hands-on technical leader or individual contributor/team member. Strong in all phases of the software development life cycle. Able to make the tradeoffs necessary to meet both product schedules and market requirements. Strong communicator. **Protocols**: IP, PPP, ATM, Frame Relay, X.25, IGMP, SNMP, (M)OSPF, PIM, DVMRP, RADIUS, Kerberos, X9.17, X/Ymodem, proprietary. **I/O Drivers**: Async/RS232 (Unix TERMIO, Windows, Macintosh, M68302 SCC, Intel 8250/16550A), disk, printer, display, front panel display and keypad for various data encryptors, smart module devices. **Operating Systems**: Unix, PSOS, MS-DOS, Windows, MAC, VMS, proprietary. **Development Environments**: Clearcase, Unix, Linux, Windows/NT, MS-DOS, GNU, PC-Based Cross Compilers, In-Circuit Emulators, Protocol Analyzers, PC-Simulation, GDB, Cisco routers. **Languages**: C (15 yrs), C++ (5 yrs), Assembler (Intel 80x86/i960, Motorola 68k)

Experience

Lucent/Ascend/Cascade Communications   Software Engineer
Westford, MA   6/96 to 10/01

In the IP Switching/Routing group, architect/lead implementer of Policy-Based Forwarding feature allowing IP packets to be selectively forwarded over cut-through Policy (QoS) PVCs. There were 3 parts to this feature: 1) the creation and maintenance of the distributed/replicated policy database, 2) the establishment of the QoS PVCs which supported ingress/egress port types of IP over ATM, Frame Relay, PPP and Ethernet, and 3) the selective forwarding of data over those PVCs.

Took on the responsibility of all new multicast routing protocol development that included debugging and making major enhancements (configuration, support for SSM) to an existing implementation of the PIM protocol. Also implemented IGMP V2 and helped troubleshoot software defects in other multicast protocols (MOSPF and DVMRP).

Other tasks included: enhancements to TCP/IP BSD stack (sockets, mbufs); implementation of a debug trace facility for IP, SNMP and PPP packets; implementation of SNMP agents/MIBs and console CLI configuration for: IGMP, PIM, Policy-Based-Forwarding and RADIUS client; implementation of CLI configuration for OSPF; implementation of a logging server.

All work done on Frame Relay and ATM multi-processor embedded platforms. (C/C++, Intel I960 assembler)

Self Employed   Contract Software Engineer
Acton, MA   8/89 to 6/96

Cascade Communications: For Cascade's Frame Relay/ATM switches, implemented/enhanced the following PPP protocols: LCP, IPCP, MLPPP, PAP/CHAP and BAP. Additionally, implemented client side of RADIUS Authentication protocol. (embedded C/C++) (9 months)

DEC: For DEC's embedded M68000-based remote network access product, implemented client side of RADIUS Authentication protocol. (7 months)

Sun Microsystems: For Sun's PC-based IP network access product, ported client side of Kerberos Authentication protocol and numerous network utilities including RCP, RSH, RLOGIN, and PING. (5 months)

Thomson Financial Services: Implemented a multi-port Asynchronous Connection Manager allowing DOS, Windows and Macintosh Clients to communicate with a Unix Server over dial-up links. This provided the above platforms with 1) a common socket-like API for the management of connections, 2) a script engine for the establishment and termination of dial-up connections, 3) a point-to-point protocol for the reliable delivery of data, and 4) low-level I/O interfaces to a variety of port types for the above mentioned platforms (MAC, DOS, Windows and Unix). Also implemented interrupt-driven 8250/16550A device driver. (12 months)

DEC: Led a project to improve the performance and reliability of an M68000-based Statistical Multiplexor. Increased throughput by a factor of 20. (5 months)

Technical Communications Corporation: Implemented Async Connection Services allowing a Unix-based Network Management System to dial up and carry on diagnostic/key distribution sessions with M68302-based data encryptors. For both the Unix and embedded platforms this included: 1) an Open/Close/Snd/Rcv API for the management of connections, 2) modem dial/answer services, 3) a reliable data link protocol, and 4) low level I/O interfaces (Unix TERMIO, M68302 device driver). Implemented FIPS-140 compliant version of X9.17 Encryption Key Distribution Protocol. Implemented firmware for an M68000-based modem-implant board providing encryption services for a Radio Packet Switching Modem. (3 1/2 years)

Technical Communications Corporation   Lead Software Engineer/Manager
Concord, MA   9/85 to 7/89

Designed/participated in implementation of a number of M68000-based real-time data encryptors (IP/X.25/sync/async). Implemented a number of point-to-point Key Encryption protocols and real-time communications executives which were responsible for: 1) bi-directional encryption of data, 2) scheduling/executing automatic Encryption Key changes, 3) servicing diagnostic/key management requests from another data encryptor or from a Key Management Station, 4) scheduling/running background diagnostics, 5) logging and reporting errors/alarms, and 6) servicing the encryptor's front panel keypad and display.

Education - B.A. Modern Languages, University of Maryland (3 years completed). Computer Science courses taken at Boston University. Conversant in German and Spanish.

Appendix II – Coding Example

```
/*
 *
 *
 *                         -- EasyComm --
 *
 *                    Disk Capture File Functions
 *
 *
 * While in 'on-line' interactive dialogue mode, all characters received may
 * be logged into a file named "RECEIVE.LOG" which can then be accessed
 * by all DOS file commands such as "TYPE", "RENAME" and "DEL".
 * This module contains the low level functions for accessing the Disk
 * Capture (log) file.
 *
 *
 *         dcf_open   - open the Disk Capture File
 *         dcf_put    - put a byte to the Disk Capture File
 *         dcf_clos   - close the Disk Capture File
 *
 */

#include    "ec_defn.c"
#include    "ec_xtern.c"

#define     LGBSIZ 512

extern      char dc_name[];              /* name of Disk Capture file       */

char        dc_buff[LGBSIZ];             /* file write buffer               */
char        dc_file = 'N';               /* log file is NOT open            */
int         dc_fid;                      /* file id of log file             */
int         dc_dsp;                      /* displacement into write buffer  */
char        dc_last = 0;                 /* last char received              */
```

```
/*
 * DCF_OPEN function
 *
 * Calling Procedure:
 *
 *              dcf_open()
 *
 * Description:
 *
 * The Disk Capture file is opened if logging is enabled and if it is not
 * already open. If there is an error opening the file, it is reported.
 *
 */

dcf_open()

{
if (dc_file EQ 'Y') return;              /* file already open                      */
dc_fid = file_opn(dc_name,WCMODE);      /* open/create for write, append         */
if (dc_fid LT 0)                         /* open error                            */
   {
   dlog_err();                           /* report the problem                    */
   return;
   }
dc_file = 'Y';                           /* log is open                           */
dc_dsp = 0;                              /* current displacement into log buf*/
return;
}
```

```
/*
 * DCF_PUT function
 *
 * Calling Procedure:
 *
 *              dcf_put(byte)
 *                      byte = byte to write to Disk Capture File
 *
 * Description:
 *
 * The byte is put to the log write buffer. Once the buffer is full it
 * is written to disk. If there is a file write error, the caller is told
 * and logging is disabled.
 *
 */

dcf_put(byte)

char      byte;

{
int       stat;

if (dc_file EQ 'N') return;                /* the file is not open            */

if (dc_last EQ 0x0D AND byte EQ 0x0A)      /* ignore lfeed after carr ret     */
  return;

dc_buff[dc_dsp] = byte;                    /* byte to file write buffer       */
dc_dsp++;                                  /* file write buffer ptr           */
if (dc_dsp EQ LGBSIZ)                      /* buffer full                     */
  {
  dc_dsp = 0;                              /* file write buffer now empty     */
  stat = file_wt(dc_fid,dc_buff,LGBSIZ);   /* write out the buffer            */
  if (stat NE 0)                           /* write error                     */
    {
    dlog_err();                            /* tell user                       */
    dcf_clos();                            /* close it                        */
    return;
    }
  }
if (byte EQ 0x0D)                          /* this was a CR                   */
  {
  ...
  }
dc_last = byte;                            /* last byte received              */
return;
}
```

```
/*
 * DCF_CLOS function
 *
 * Calling Procedure:
 *
 *          dcf_clos()
 *
 * Description:
 *
 * The Disk Capture File is closed. If there are bytes in the write buffer,
 * they are written before the close.
 *
 */

dcf_clos()

{
if (dc_file EQ 'Y')                            /* log is open             */
  {
  if (dc_dsp GT 0)                             /* bytes in log buffer     */
     file_wt(dc_fid,dc_buff,dc_dsp);           /* write out the bytes     */
  file_cls(dc_fid);                            /* close the file          */
  dc_file = 'N';                               /* log is closed           */
  }
return;
}
```

```
/*
 * Following are functions local to this module
 */

/*
 * DLOG_ERR function
 *
 * Calling Procedure:
 *
 *         dlog_err()
 *
 * Description:
 *
 * This function is to be called if there is a disk log access failure.
 * The caller is informed and the necessary cleanup steps taken.
 *
 * A normal error message cannot be used as there is info on the error
 * line that cannot be disturbed.
 *
 */

dlog_err()

{
beep();
dsk_fail();                          /* DISK_LOG FAILURE message */
logging_off();                       /* turn off logging         */
return;
}
```